SCIENCE, TECHNOLOGY, AND SOCIETY

THE POLITICS OF HOUSING INNOVATION

The Fate of the Civilian Industrial Technology Program

THE POLITICS OF HOUSING INNOVATION

*The Fate of the
Civilian Industrial Technology Program*

DOROTHY NELKIN

Cornell University Press

ITHACA AND LONDON

To Lisa and Laurie

Acknowledgments

This is the second book to be written under the auspices of the Cornell University Program on Science, Technology, and Society. I have relied heavily on the cooperation of participants in the controversy described in this book and on others with knowledge bearing on particular aspects of the case. These include Allan Astin, Harvey Brooks, Joseph A. Carreiro, Clarence H. Danhof, John Eberhard, Gordon P. Fisher, Jerome E. Hass, Barbara Hinckley, J. Herbert Hollomon, Samuel A. Lawrence, Franklin A. Long, Michael Michaelis, Richard R. Nelson, David Ragone, Richard A. Rettig, Robert Stern, and Douglas Whitlock. The book could not have been written without their cooperation in telephone and personal interviews, the documentary material and references they provided, and their extensive criticism of various drafts of the manuscript. Sharon Bryan and Sidney Siskin made significant contributions through their editorial and research assistance. Finally, I am indebted to the National Science Foundation and the Sloan Foundation for supporting the research and writing of this study.

Dorothy Nelkin

Ithaca, New York

Contents

Tables

THE POLITICS OF HOUSING INNOVATION

*The Fate of the Civilian
Industrial Technology Program*

Introduction

Among the basic social questions facing science and science-based technology today are questions of the extent to which science and technology are relevant to the definition and resolution of the mix of urban and racial problems of the United States, of the extent to which the priorities of what is loosely termed federal science policy can be restructured to express a commitment to the restoration of decent urban life. . . .[1]

Although federal research and development activities have been largely confined to the defense and space industries, scientists and technologists have increasingly sought ways to apply their knowledge to urgent problems in the civilian sector. Their efforts have encountered formidable obstacles. A number of issues remain to be resolved if the enormous technical capabilities of the nation are to be reoriented to socially desirable ends. How, for example, is the transfer of technology from the defense and space industries to the civilian economy to be effected? How are those with a vested interest in the

[1] James D. Carroll, "Science and the City: The Question of Authority," *Science*, 163, February 28, 1969, p. 903.

status quo to be dealt with? Can scientists and technologists adapt themselves to the demands of practical politics, and what are the likely consequences if they cannot? What agencies—public or private—should be in charge of directing and applying technological developments to domestic social problems? These and other complex questions came to the fore in the controversy over the Civilian Industrial Technology Program (CITP). The history of that important and finally abortive program shows clearly the difficulties involved in any attempt to restructure federal research and development policy to respond to social needs.

The controversy began in 1962 when J. Herbert Hollomon, assistant secretary for science and technology in the Department of Commerce, requested congressional appropriations for the proposed CITP.[2] The program had three primary aims: (1) to foster innovation in "lagging" industries, including building and textiles; (2) to study the information needs and the state of technology in other industries; and (3) to create an industry-university service to diffuse information and provide technical aid.

The CITP proposal embodied a general concern, at the executive level of government, with technology and economic growth in the civilian sector—a concern expressed in a search for ways to stimulate innovation through the transfer of existing scientific and technolog-

---

[2] Hollomon appeared before the Subcommittee on Deficiencies of the Committee on Appropriations, House of Representatives, August 1962.

ical knowledge from defense and space to civilian industry. The basic question was, simply: How do you increase research and development in an area of the economy which would benefit from improved technology? Backers of the CITP were convinced that free-market mechanisms could not provide an optimal allocation of research and development (R&D) resources and that federal programs were required to do the job.

The CITP was never fully funded, though an appropriation was made to support, for a limited time, that part of the program involving the textiles industry. The proposals relating to the building industry met immediate and vehement opposition, however, and sparked most of the controversy that eventually brought about the collapse of the entire program. For this reason, the building industry is the focus of the present study.

The building industry was included in the CITP because—despite the availability of new materials and new means of mass production [3]—the pace of change in construction methods did not appear sufficient to meet the acute and increasing need for adequate shelter at reasonable cost. Proponents of the CITP, noting rising construction costs and continuing housing shortages, sought to stimulate greater research and development in the building industry through federal activity. Their effort was complicated by the fact that the usefulness of R&D for solving problems of the cost and quantity of housing had never been demonstrated. Considering the urgency

[3] Donald A. Schon, *Technology and Change* (New York: Delta, 1967), pp. 156ff.

of the situation, however, and the very limited amount of R&D work being done in the industry, a gain from federal investment appeared almost certain.

Why did the CITP fail? The program offered to assist an industry in realizing its technological potential. Intended to resolve the industry's problem in keeping pace with expanding housing needs, its objectives were supported by the Kennedy administration. Significant improvement in construction methods was technologically possible, given a systematic program directed to this end. A model for a successful large-scale technological program existed in the space and defense industries. Moreover, the proposal was made at a time when public opinion was highly receptive to technological solutions to problems. The public showed little of the skepticism concerning technology that was to develop several years later. As we will see, the explanation of the program's failure must be sought in the response of the building industry and its political spokesmen to the threats—real or imagined—posed by technological innovation and in the inherent conservatism of the political process.

The study begins with a brief description of the building industry in the early 1960's, then takes up the pattern of federal research and development activities at that time, as well as the discussions and documents that provided the impetus for developing the CITP. Next, the reception, modification, and eventual demise of the CITP are examined in relation to the participating individuals and institutions. Finally, some of the general issues and implications of the case are analyzed.

I / The Building Industry and the Federal Government

The Building Industry

All economic conditions indicate that the nation is now entering on several decades of unprecedented and accelerating growth . . . which could call for a total output of structures before the end of this century at least equal to our total current inventory. . . . To meet a future of tremendous challenge and to utilize a huge but not clearly defined potential, a coordinated way must be found to . . . devise methods and techniques through which continuing growth and development can be assured.[1]

The premise behind the CITP proposal was that technological activity in the building industry was simply not sufficient to meet the unprecedented need for new construction. The industry is very large, though estimates of its size vary, depending on whether heavy-construction and maintenance costs are included. Esti-

---

[1] Building Research Advisory Board, *A Program for Building Research in the United States: A Report to the National Bureau of Standards* (April 5, 1962).

mates for 1961–1962 ranged from $40 billion annually (or 7.5 per cent of the GNP) to $80 billion annually (or 16 per cent of the GNP).[2] But despite its size, productivity in the construction industry has increased at a significantly slower rate than the economy as a whole.[3] A 1963 study by the Columbia University Bureau of Applied Social Research measured, by output per worker, the growth in productivity of United States industries between 1950 and 1960. Various industries were ranked as shown in Table 1. Note that a consistent annual growth rate of less than 2 per cent is characteristic primarily of service industries.

The rate of productivity growth in construction was attributed not to lack of market demand but to "technological lag." A 1963 study by Arthur D. Little, Inc., on innovation in the use of technological resources by five "mature" industries asserted that "during the last thirty years there has been no major technological change of

[2] The BRAB report (*op. cit.*) estimated that building in 1961 in the United States involved more than $80 billion annually, or 16% of the GNP.

A. D. Little, Inc., *Patterns and Problems of Technical Innovation in American Industry: Report to National Science Foundation, U.S. Department of Commerce* (September 1963), indicates the building industry is a $40 billion a year industry—7.5% of the GNP.

The White House Panel on Civilian Technology, Executive Office of the President, U.S. Office of Science and Technology, *Better Housing for the Future* (April 1963), estimated that it represents nearly $60 billion annually, or about 11% of the GNP.

[3] John W. Kendrick, *Productivity Trends in the United States* (Princeton: Princeton University Press, 1961), pp. 489–494.

major economic significance for the building industry.
. . . Technological change has been primarily evolutionary in small increments, significant only in the aggre-
gate. . . . It can hardly be called 'innovation.' " [4]

Table 1. Productivity growth in selected industries,
1950–1960 *

Growth of more than 5% per year
    Electric utilities
    Aircraft and parts
    Chemicals
    Air lines

Growth of 4% to 4.9% per year
    Agriculture
    Textile mills

Growth of 3% to 3.9% per year
    Food manufacture
    Rubber
    Lumber

Growth of 2% to 2.9% per year
    Real estate sales
    Stone, clay and glass products
    Medical services
    Construction

Growth of 1% to 1.9% per year
    Restaurants
    Insurance
    Personal services
    Fabricated metal products

---

* *Source: Business Week*, September 14, 1963, p. 188.
This ranking measures output per worker. A more
precise ranking would have to include hours worked.

[4] Arthur D. Little, Inc., *op. cit.*, p. 133.

There are several measures of the attitude of an industry toward technological innovation. One is the amount of funds its spends for R&D. During the early 1960's the ratio of R&D to value-added in the construction industry was .12, in contrast with .43 in the economy as a whole.[5] In 1956 the funds actually spent for R&D by the construction industry, compared with those of several other industries, were estimated as follows: [6]

Construction	$ 24,100,000
Chemical	517,700,000
Electrical Equipment	461,000,000
Machinery	390,300,000
Aircraft	269,900,000

The $24.1 million spent by the construction industry represents only that spent by contractors and therefore excludes the amount put into production development by building-material manufacturers. But product manufacturers also spent less on R&D relative to their sales than manufacturers as a whole.[7]

By the early 1960's, all industries in the United States were estimated to have spent an average of 1.5 per cent

[5] Richard R. Nelson, Merton J. Peck, Edward D. Kalachek, *Technology, Economic Growth and Public Policy* (Washington, D.C.: Brookings Institution, 1967), p. 193.

[6] Glenn H. Beyer, *Housing and Society* (New York: Macmillan, 1965), p. 492.

[7] Kendrick, *op. cit.*, p. 182. While all manufacturing industries spent 1.18% of their total sales on R&D, the figure for lumber producers was 3.77%.

of their gross sales income on R&D. If it were to match the average industrial practice, the building industry, with an estimated $24 billion in sales of new buildings annually, would have had to spend about $400 million on R&D. Only a very small fraction of that amount was so used.

One further indication of an industry's technological effort is the number of scientists and research engineers it employs; in 1960 the number employed by our selected industries was as follows: [8]

Construction	2,000
Chemical	36,000
Electrical Equipment	62,600
Machinery	28,200
Aircraft	64,000

With limited R&D activity, technological change in the construction industry was diffuse and incremental. Increasing labor costs were not offset by rapid technological advance either in the use of new materials or new methods of construction as they were in other industries. Although the cost of building materials increased only 18.4 per cent from 1950 to 1962,[9] the lack of industrial innovation was reflected in a dramatic rise in construc-

[8] National Science Foundation, *Scientific and Technical Personnel in Industry, 1960.* (Report 61–75, Washington, D.C.: GPO, 1961).

[9] Beyer, *op. cit.,* p. 240.

tion costs, disproportionate to changes in the Consumer Price Index (see Table 2).

The problem of technological innovation must be examined with respect to the organization of the industry and its methods of production. Perhaps the most important source of technological lag was the compartmentalized character of the industry. The industry has many diverse segments: contractors, architects, engineering firms, craft unions, suppliers, entrepreneurs of build-

Table 2. Construction costs and consumer price indexes, selected years, 1950–1962

Year	Construction costs	Consumer price index *
1950	111.6	102.8
1954	132.5	114.8
1958	156.0	123.5
1962	172.1	129.3

* The price index for 1947–1949 was 100.

Sources: Construction statistics are from *Engineering News Record, Building Cost Index.* They include cost of skilled labor, structural steel, cement, and lumber—20 cities' average. The consumer price index is found in U.S. Department of Labor, Bureau of Labor Statistics reports.

ing projects, laborers, brokers and realtors. Its fragmentation is apparent in Table 3, which shows the various participants and influences involved in the building process. Each segment of the building industry is itself fragmented into numerous scattered firms. For example, in

Table 3. Major participants and influences on the building process *

Participants			
Developer	Developer	Developer	Owner
Land owner	Landing institutions (interim and permanent)	Real estate brokers	Maintenance firms and employees
Lawyers	FHA, VA, or private mortgage insurance company	Lawyers	Property management firms
Real estate brokers	Contractors	Lending institutions	Insurance companies
Title companies	Subcontractors	Title companies	Utility companies
Architects and engineers	Craftsmen and their unions	FHA, VA, or private mortgage insurance company	Tax assessors
Surveyor	Material manufacturers and distributors		Repairmen, craftsmen and their unions
Planners and consultants	Building code officials		Lending institutions
	Insurance companies		Architects and engineers
	Architects and engineers		Contractors
			Subcontractors
			Material manufacturers and distributors
			Local zoning officials
			Local building officials

(1) PREPARATION → PHASE	(2) PRODUCTION → PHASE	(3) DISTRIBUTION ⇆ PHASE	(4) SERVICE PHASE
a. Land acquisitions	a. Site preparation	a. Sale (and subsequent resale or refinancing)	a. Maintenance and management
b. Planning	b. Construction		b. Repairs
c. Zoning amendments	c. Financing		c. Improvements and additions

Influences			
Real estate law	Banking laws	Recording regulations and fees	Property taxes
Recording regulations and fees	Building and mechanical codes	Real estate law	Income taxes
Banking laws	Subdivision regulations	Transfer taxes	Housing and health codes
Zoning	Utility regulations	Banking laws	Insurance laws
Subdivision regulations	Union rules	Rules of professional association	Utility regulations
Private deed restrictions	Rules of trade and professional association		Banking laws
Public master plans	Insurance laws		Union rules
	Laws controlling transportation of materials		Rules of trade and professional association
			Zoning
			Building and mechanical codes
			Laws controlling transportation of materials

* *Source:* President's Commission on Urban Housing, *A Decent Home* (Washington, D.C.: GPO, December 11, 1967).

1961 there were several hundred thousand small private "home builders," some eighty-five thousand general contractors, plus 9,800 architect and engineering firms in the United States.[10] The structure has been maintained by tradition and reinforced by natural constraints, the difficulties of land aggregation in populated areas, transportation limitations, and uncertain and fluctuating economic factors.

Small builders often operate on a handicraft basis. It is difficult for them to fund research and development. They have little risk capital and little profit motivation to engage in costly and long-term innovative activities. Small industries tend to have short-term proprietary objectives. Innovation, when it occurs, tends to be piecemeal and particularistic, limited to proprietary products. The diversity of both the products of various segments in the industry and of the needs of particular geographic areas, have worked against the development of integrated research programs.

Other constraints on technological innovation are a function of the character of "mature industries": their commitment to traditional methods and existing skills, the family structure of many segments of the industry, and a lack of entrepreneurial models.

Technological progress in the construction industry has been primarily limited to materials. There was some "invasion" of the industry by new technologically advanced industries such as plastics, but reception was

10 Arthur D. Little, Inc., *op. cit.*, p. 116.

reluctant and the impact of new technology has been minimal.[11] For example, in 1961 a proposal was developed by Arthur D. Little, Inc., for a three-year study program aimed at accelerating the use of plastics in the housing industry. At that time the plastics industry had developed materials applicable to housing. But "the cautious evolutionary or nibbling away process of introducing plastics into home building . . . [was not] a particularly fruitful method of attack." [12] The A. D. Little proposal for a study program fell through. It faced too many obstacles: "building codes which are commonly specific for conventional materials but not for performance; labor union habits and regulations; building understanding of and confidence in the materials; home buyers' likes and dislikes which are conditioned by time-honored habits and customs, the attitude of loan agencies . . . and fire insurance underwriters." [13]

The character of building codes is a major obstacle to large-scale adoption of new technology. There are about 5,000 different district codes in the United States, and

[11] Donald A. Schon, *Technology and Change* (New York: Delta, 1967), chap. 1; and Donald A. Schon, "Innovation by Invasion," *International Science and Technology*, March 1964, pp. 52ff.

[12] Nelson et al., *op. cit.*, p. 83. The introduction went only as far as the use of plastics in electrical insulation materials and paint, and to some extent in floor coverings; in 1962 only 2% of the construction material dollar was spent on plastics.

[13] Mortimer H. Nixon, "Plastics in Housing: A Program for Growth," *New Building Research* (Building Research Institute Publication 986, Spring 1961), p. 160.

regulations are usually based on specifications for material and components, seldom on performance requirements. Codes are developed primarily to ensure consumer safety, but definitions of "safety" are based on traditional criteria. For example, the required thickness of a wall is defined in terms of the character of certain materials in use at the time a code is established, although new materials may have entirely different properties that make the old criteria irrelevant.

But changes in codes are slow, constrained by vested interests and lack of technical knowledge of how to rewrite standardized codes in performance language. This has proved a deterrent to the introduction of new materials, and is therefore a major factor in the rising costs of construction. One builder of prefabricated housing at the time the CITP was proposed estimated that a national performance code would allow him to slash the price of his products by at least 25 per cent.[14]

Civilian Research and the Federal Government

The role of the federal government in civilian research and development became a crucial issue in the CITP controversy. Hollomon's arguments for federal spending were based on the gap between federal R&D expenditures for civilian activities and those for defense and space activities (see Table 4).

Two-thirds of the federal funds for R&D were contracted to private industry, but primarily for activities related to the Department of Defense, NASA, and the

[14] *Saturday Evening Post*, September 21, 1963, p. 24.

AEC.[15] This helped to create an industrial imbalance whereby, for example, in 1960, three hundred manufacturing companies in chemicals, machinery, electrical equipment, communications, and aircraft carried out over 75 per cent of total R&D performed by private industry. The aircraft industry itself accounted for over half the total industrial R&D financed by the federal government. The imbalance in the distribution of federal funds in the United States were reflected in a heavy

Table 4. Federal funds for R&D, fiscal 1962 (in billions)

Agency	*Amount*		
Department of Defense	$ 6.7	HEW	.603
NASA	1.4	Agriculture	.163
AEC	1.1	NSF	.106
All other agencies	1.1	Interior	.093
TOTAL	$10.3	FAA	.058
		Commerce	.042
		Others	.057

Source: National Science Foundation, *Federal Funds for Science* (NSF 63–11, Washington, 1963).

geographic concentration of R&D, as well as in the striking industrial concentration.[16] This situation was to continue during the 1960's. By contrast, Germany and

[15] National Science Foundation, *R&D in Industry* (NSF 64–9, Washington, 1962).

[16] Forty-one per cent of R&D funds were spent in California and 59% in the three states of California, New York, and Massachusetts in 1962.

Japan were putting about 75 per cent of their federal R&D expenditures into the private needs of the economy.[17]

This imbalance in federal R&D spending began to develop following World War II and, after the launching of Sputnik in 1957, increased significantly with the growth of NASA's budget and continued expansion in defense spending. Major congressional appropriations for NASA were made after President Kennedy's 1961 statement that the United States would be first to land a man on the moon.

The resulting distribution of scientific and technical manpower and its possible consequences for economic productivity in neglected sectors became, in the early 1960's, a matter of considerable concern to the group of scientists and technologists brought together by President Kennedy to establish the guidelines for science policy.

In his *Economic Report to Congress* for 1962, Kennedy asserted that government has the responsibility for "maintaining a suitable environment for private research and for supporting programs which are in the public interest which are not adequately stimulated by private market opportunities." [18] He emphasized the importance

[17] Edwin Mansfield, *The Economics of Technological Change* (New York: W. W. Norton, 1968), p. 164.

[18] President John F. Kennedy, *Economic Report to Congress 1962*, quoted in Subcommittee for Departments of State, Justice and Commerce of the Committee on Appropriations, House of Representatives, 88th Congress, First Session, *Hearings on the Department of Commerce* (Washington, D.C.: GPO, 1964), p. 792.

of research to the civilian economy, hoping to "encourage civilian research and development and make the by-products of military and space research easily accessible to civilian industry." [19] In his *Budget Message* of January 1962 he noted that "the defense, space and atomic energy activities of the country absorb about two-thirds of the trained people. . . . We have paid a price by sharply limiting the scarce scientific and engineering research available to civilian sectors of the economy. . . . I believe the federal government must now redress the balance." [20] Kennedy's statements led to considerable discussion about the criteria for government support of civilian R&D in a number of areas. A set of general guidelines was recommended by a group that was concerned not with housing but with the development and utilization of energy resources. These criteria suggested that the government should be active in cases where:

1. The results of research, though of definite social benefit, may be such that, because of externalities, the private firm is unable to capture enough of the value of the total social benefits to recoup its costs.
2. The beneficial results of research may not be expected until a time so far in the future that those benefits will be discounted by the private firm at a rate of discount greater than the appropriate rate for society. For this reason, the private firm may assign to a research endeavor with distant payoff a smaller present value than the present value for society.

[19] *Congressional Quarterly*, January 25, 1963, p. 82.
[20] John F. Kennedy, *Budget Message 1962.*

3. The range of possible returns to a given research program may be so great and reflect so much uncertainty that, if the program calls for a major outlay, a private firm may be unwilling to embark upon it because of risk aversion and its inability to diversify its research portfolio adequately.[21]

Groundwork for the CITP: Discussion and Documents

President Kennedy's concern with technology and civilian industry was in large measure a product of growing pressure from his advisers, consultants, and the Council of Economic Advisers (CEA) to study the impact of civilian technology on economic growth and to seek ways of bringing appropriate existing technology into the service of private industry.

In a special message in 1961 on housing and community development Kennedy set forth his goals: "to provide decent housing for all our people and to encourage a prosperous and efficient construction industry as an essential component of general economic prosperity and growth." [22] Two days later the president lunched with Luther Hodges, secretary of the Department of Commerce, to discuss what that department could do to implement these goals. Then, in July 1961, Kennedy wrote a letter to David Bell, director of the Bureau of the Budget (BOB), requesting that the bureau and other agencies review federal government policy on contracts with private enterprise, so as to increase R&D directed

[21] Energy Studies Group, *Energy R&D and National Progress* (Washington, D.C.: GPO, 1964), pp. 71–72.

[22] "White House Special Message on Housing and Community Development," March 9, 1961.

toward public purposes. The subsequent BOB re-examination of policy in this area concluded with recommendations that the government broaden the arrangements through which it could "mobilize the talent and facilities needed" to carry out its R&D effort.[23]

On February 21, 1961, John Kenneth Galbraith and Jerome Wiesner sent a draft memorandum to the president recommending the establishment of a civilian development commission to stimulate the growth of those civilian industries "without any organized stimulus to change." They pointed to areas in the civilian economy, such as housing and transportation, where technology remained unemployed and suggested the formation of a committee, which would include the secretary of commerce, the chairman of the Council of Economic Advisers, the special assistant for science and technology, and individuals "with an affirmative view of life," to develop mechanisms to come to grips with the problem. They also recommended forming subcommittees to investigate particular industries and indicated that congressional preparation and full legislative authorization should be sought to implement the organizational recommendations of the committee.[24]

Also in early 1961, began a series of discussions involving Richard Nelson from the RAND Corporation

[23] Clarence H. Danhof, *Government Contracting and Technological Change* (Washington, D.C.: Brookings Institution, 1968), pp. 118–120.

[24] The memoranda and other material were made available to me by John Kenneth Galbraith and Jerome Wiesner.

and a staff member of the CEA; Kenneth Arrow and William Capron, from the CEA; Samuel A. Lawrence, a Bureau of the Budget examiner; and Michael Michaelis of Arthur D. Little, Inc., a consultant to Jerome Wiesner. These discussions resulted in several forward-looking memoranda sent to the president between 1961 and 1963 dealing with the environment, energy needs and fuel resources, and housing and urban problems—subjects which were not to receive widespread attention until five years later.

In addition, in their *Annual Report* of January 1962 the CEA urged Congress to enact a pending administrative bill to create the post of assistant secretary of commerce for science and technology, whose task would be to develop programs for extending research benefits to industries that lacked a research tradition.[25] This post was to be held by J. Herbert Hollomon as of May 1962. The CEA report of 1962 emphasized that technical advance was of crucial importance for economic growth, and recommended federal support to provide additional resources to the civilian market and to direct the "offspring of military research" toward civilian technology. The construction industry was identified as a target.

In the summer of 1961, the president, closely following the recommendation of the Galbraith-Wiesner memorandum, appointed a White House Panel on Civilian Technology to study the technological needs of the civilian economy and to act as a catalyst in persuading

[25] *The Annual Report of the Council of Economic Advisers* (1962) (Washington, D.C.: GPO, 1963), pp. 157ff.

various agencies to take over specific programs. A committee of three—Jerome Wiesner, who had been appointed the president's special assistant for science and technology in March 1961; Walter Heller, chairman of the Council of Economic Advisers; and Luther Hodges, the secretary of commerce—was formed. They were advised by a panel directed by Milton Harris, vice-president for research for Gillette and a chemist with considerable experience in research in the textile industry. Michael Michaelis was executive secretary.

A subpanel on housing was formed, chaired by R. A. Charpie from Union Carbide Corporation. In a report which was to have direct bearing on the development of the CITP, the subpanel stated that development of new technology must be stimulated by "a concern for the public interest rather than by the incentive for private profit alone. . . . If a major federal government science and experiment program had been started some years ago, knowledge and techniques for evaluating the worthiness of the radical innovations which were clearly predictable would now be at hand." [26] The subpanel concluded that it was appropriate for government to be involved in establishing performance criteria to stimulate and evaluate innovation, in conducting research to develop data and techniques, in supporting a study of the regulatory

[26] White House Panel, *op. cit.*, p. 10. Members of the Panel were R. A. Charpie from Union Carbide, R. M. Dillion from BRAB, J. E. Lash from ACTION, Inc., M. Meyerson from M.I.T.–Harvard Joint Center for Urban Studies, and C. F. Rassweiler from Johns Manville Corporation.

system, and in gathering information. The government's own housing-procurement activities, particularly in the Department of Defense, were recommended as a living laboratory for technological innovation. The report also advocated government support of college and university programs that involved interdisciplinary efforts to gather information relevant to building-industry technology and to train professionals to utilize new scientific information.

Explorations of the industrial-technological dilemma were also made in nongovernmental quarters. One document, later to be a source of controversy, was prepared by the Building Research Advisory Board (BRAB),[27] a committee of the National Research Council of the National Academy of Sciences. The report was prepared under the chairmanship of Richard G. Folsom, president of Rensselaer Polytechnic Institute, and subsequently a member of the National Academy of Engineering and a member-at-large of the National Research Council.

BRAB was formally established in 1949 by a committee composed of industry and government people who were seeking to develop a nongovernmental body to explore, stimulate, and coordinate research and technology in the construction industry. Douglas Whitlock, a fifty-nine-year-old Washington attorney representing Structural Clay Products Institute and the Producers' Council,[28] was instrumental in forming BRAB, using industrial

[27] BRAB, *op. cit.*

[28] These two organizations are trade associations for building industry manufacturers.

financing. The purpose was to counter the accusation by government officials that research in the construction industry lacked coordination, and the proposal in the Housing Act of 1949 that government engage in research. Also involved in the formation of BRAB was the Construction Industry Advisory Council of the United States Chamber of Commerce.[29] One of BRAB's first officers, appointed by Whitlock, was William Scheick. At the time the CITP was proposed he was executive vice-president of the American Institute of Architects, and so became a key participant in the controversy.

In 1962 the chairman of BRAB was Richard H. Tatlow, III, a national officer of the American Society of Civil Engineers. BRAB membership that year included the director of Structural Clay Products Research Foundation, Robert B. Taylor, and A. Allan Bates, of the Building Research Division of the National Bureau of Standards. Of its twenty-nine members, twenty were from industry, six from government, and three from universities (see Appendix III).

The fact that many members of BRAB are in leadership positions in professional associations or in other organizations related to the construction industry gives the organization considerable political "clout." Yet BRAB membership is based on a narrowly defined perception of the actual diversity of the building industry, including primarily those directly involved in architecture, materials production, and construction. Repre-

[29] *Architectural Record*, 105, February and April 1949.

sentatives of other crucial dimensions of the industry, such as finance and investment, science and advanced systems technology, and labor, are notably absent.

Both A. Allan Bates and William Scheick were on the special committee which wrote the BRAB report or, as it was called, the "Folsom Report." This document appeared in April 1962—prior to the CITP proposal—and was prepared in response to a request to the National Academy from the National Bureau of Standards, which was seeking to expand its competence in the area of building technology.

The report did not consider such broad concepts as were suggested by the CITP; its recommendations were limited to activities within the National Bureau of Standards (NBS). It discussed the research needs of the building industry, and did not question the existing organization of the industry beyond indicating that it impeded significant R&D activities. Because existing federal agencies were not equipped to establish a national program for housing research, the report recommended the creation of a National Institute of Building Research within the NBS, but with separate appropriation and administration. The institute would include an information service, stimulate and support research programs, and fund institutions and projects through grants and contracts. It would also do some internal research. Financial support of $2 million for the first year was recommended, to be increased in time to $6 million.

The findings of the BRAB report satisfied neither the conservative element of the building industry nor those who sought a radically new approach to building technology. Industry representatives claimed that the report did not speak for private industry. As a consequence of the report, BRAB itself was criticized as an originally prestigious organization that had deteriorated due to its complacency during the favorable climate of the Eisenhower administration. But after the CITP was proposed, the recommendations of the BRAB report were to find favor with many industry representatives who preferred activity within the predictable setting of the National Bureau of Standards to the creation of an independent agency.

An important document supporting the CITP appeared in December 1962—a proposal by Arthur D. Little, Inc., for a pilot study on problems of technological innovation in five U.S. industries, including textiles and construction. The industries were to be studied for their general characteristics, dominant patterns of innovation, and internal obstacles to innovation. The findings of this study, which had been encouraged by Hollomon, appeared in a report to the National Science Foundation in September 1963 by Donald Schon, then at Arthur D. Little, Inc., and later director of the Department of Commerce, Office of Technical Services. The report recommended a program to foster transfer of existing technology to the building industry, modeled on the experience of the Agricultural Extension Program. The government's role in this effort would be to act "neither as a monitor nor a crutch, but a partner in technological change on the grounds of representing interests broader than those of an individual company, industry, group of workers or area of the country."[30]

Related to this study, a conference on the problems and patterns of technical innovation was held in March 1963 to explore problems of innovation and questions concerning organizational structure with respect to R&D activities. The conference also took up the question of immediate concern to Hollomon in planning the CITP, namely, the desirability and feasibility of federal government help with the problems of technical innovation in industry. Several models were presented of possible programs in which the government would act as a "supracorporate organization." The conference concluded that a new pattern of government-industry collaboration was desirable, with the government acting as a facilitating and catalytic agent in encouraging technical competence.[31]

In sum, the CITP was supported by two categories of material. First, policy statements and reports from the Bureau of the Budget, the White House, and the Council of Economic Advisers, declared the need for government activity in the area of civilian technology. These were motivated by an economic policy of rapid growth, a faith in technology, and a recognition of the inadequacies of market mechanisms to dictate optimal allocation of technological resources. Second, there were proposals

[30] Arthur D. Little, Inc., *op. cit.*, p. 200.

[31] Donald Schon, *Problems of Innovation in American Industry*, Report to the U.S. Department of Commerce (Arthur D. Little, Inc., May 1963).

suggesting possible organizational forms for new R&D activity, the most specific being the BRAB proposal for a National Institute for Building Research and Schon's model of an extension-type program. These documents laid the foundation for the CITP.

II / The Civilian Industrial Technology Program

The Department of Commerce and
J. Herbert Hollomon

The statutory functions of the Department [of Commerce]
are to foster, promote and develop the foreign and domestic
commerce, the manufacturing and shipping industries, and
the transportation facilities of the United States.[1]

The Department of Commerce has traditionally been a
spokesman for business and industry, responding to business needs and encouraging their representation in government by such trade associations as the Chamber of
Commerce. With this orientation, the department has
generally been bypassed in new government activities
that would increase public control over economic life.[2]
Thus the proposal for a Civilian Industrial Technology

[1] Secretary of Commerce, *Annual Report* (Washington, D.C.:
U.S. Department of Commerce, 1963).

[2] Theodore J. Lowi, *The End of Liberalism* (New York:
W. W. Norton, 1969), pp. 119–120.

Program within the department was clearly a deviation from the department's traditional relationship with civilian industry.

The department has generally not fared well in appropriations requests, and from 1947 to 1962 it suffered reductions in budget estimates disproportionate to those of other departments. See, for example, Table 5, in which House appropriations in commerce are compared with those in agriculture.

Table 5. House Appropriations Committee decisions on budget requests, 1947–1962

Decision	*Department of Commerce (five bureaus)*	*Department of Agriculture (five bureaus)*
Increase	1 (1.2%)	17 (25.5%)
Leave the same	6 (7.5%)	15 (19.0%)
Decrease	73 (91.3%)	47 (59.5%)

Source: Richard F. Fenno, *The Power of the Purse* (Boston: Little Brown, 1966), pp. 363–65.

From 1949 to 1959, the budget for all federal nondefense science and technology increased at an annual rate of about 2.5 times that of the Department of Commerce.[3] The difficulties of that department in garnering adequate financial support were reflected in the relatively small increase in its R&D activities, which, during the same period, it could not even double.

[3] National Academy of Sciences, *Role of the Department of Commerce in Science and Technology* (Washington, D.C.: GPO, March 1960).

Concerned with this situation and its implications for economic growth, in 1960 a panel of the National Academy of Sciences recommended reorganization of the Department of Commerce and the establishment of a position of assistant secretary for science and technology. This recommendation was supported by the Council of Economic Advisers (CEA) and by Jerome Wiesner when he became the president's special assistant for science and technology in March 1961. Wiesner was attempting to develop scientific and engineering competence at high policy levels, in order to activate a government role in stimulating technological innovation in industries that had failed to make substantial investment in R&D.[4] Supported by the CEA and the White House Panel on Civilian Technology, Wiesner wanted the Department of Commerce to develop a pilot program that would be helpful in elaborating a proper long-term federal role to foster economic growth through institutional and technological change.

The position of assistant secretary of science and technology in the Department of Commerce was established by congressional legislation in February 1962. The new post was intended to coordinate the scientific and technological programs of the Department of Commerce, its main objective being to relate these programs effectively to economic and industrial growth. The post was

[4] Jerome Wiesner, "Statement on Research Development in the National Interest," *Hearings Before the Select Committee on Government Research* (House of Representatives, 88th Congress, November 1963), p. 262.

filled in May 1962 by J. Herbert Hollomon, who was
then a general manager of the General Engineering
Laboratories of the General Electric Company. Jerome
Wiesner was instrumental in the selection of Hollomon,
who, at the time of his appointment, was involved in
government activities as a consultant to the President's
Science Advisory Committee and a member of a federal
panel concerned with the transfer of technology to
underdeveloped countries.

Hollomon's activities indicated a general concern with
the technological needs of the civilian economy that was
consistent with the developing policy of the administration. In 1962, as chairman of the Engineering Research
Committee of the Engineers Joint Council (representing
major U.S. engineering societies), Hollomon had organized a study group to assess the changing needs of
society. One of the many concerns of this group was
urban problems, and a panel headed by R. G. Folsom
(author of the BRAB report) recommended that the
council set up ties with the President's Science Advisory
Committee for the purpose of defining the problems that
were amenable to a technological approach.[5] It was the
research committee's far-reaching analysis of technological needs that brought Hollomon to the attention of
Jerome Wiesner and the group in Washington concerned with scientific and technical policy issues.

Hollomon had long experience in technical administration and the development of applied research.

[5] Engineers Joint Council, *The Nation's Engineering Research Needs, 1965–1985* (May 25, 1962).

Dr. John Herbert Hollomon was born in Norfolk, Va., on March 12, 1919. He received his B.S. and D. Sc. degrees from the Massachusetts Institute of Technology.

Dr. Hollomon served as a metallurgical engineer with the Revere Copper & Brass Co. in 1940; as a research associate at the Massachusetts Institute of Technology in 1940–41; and as an instructor in the Graduate School of Engineering of Harvard University in 1941–42.

Dr. Hollomon [had] been associated with the General Electric Co. since 1946; becoming manager of the metallurgy and ceramics research department in 1952. Since 1960 he [had] been general manager of the General Engineering Laboratory of the Company.

Dr. Hollomon [was] a member of the Development Assistance Panel and the Scientific and Technological Manpower Panel of the President's Science Advisory Committee; chairman of the Engineering Research Committee of the Engineers Joint Council; member of the U.S. Army's Scientific Advisory Panel; and member of the Commission on Engineering Education. . . .

In education, Dr. Hollomon [had] been an adjunct professor of metallurgy at Rensselaer Polytechnic Institute and [had] served in advisory educational posts at Cornell, Harvard, and the Massachusetts Institute of Technology.[6]

Hollomon's position as a technical administrator at General Electric immediately prior to his joining the Department of Commerce required ideas, technical com-

---

[6] "Biographical Sketch of J. Herbert Hollomon," Committee on Commerce, U.S. Senate, 87th Congress, Second Session, *Hearings on Sundry Nominations*, February 1962 (Washington, D.C.: GPO), pp. 149–50.

petence, the ability to organize research, "to get the right man working on the right problem at the right time and in the right way," [7] and also salesmanship. "The last two years I had the responsibility for the central engineering organization that has as its responsibility the generation of new business for the company from a technological point of view. We were supposed to ask the question, What are the new products the public, the consumer will buy, and how do we go about developing these products?" [8]

Hollomon's new position carried responsibility for the National Bureau of Standards, the Coast and Geodetic Survey, the Patent Office, the Weather Bureau, and the Office of Technical Services. This involved him in fostering new activities intended to strengthen the National Bureau of Standards—still recovering from the battery additive controversy of 1953—and in reorganizing the Patent Examining Corps and the Weather Bureau Meteorological satellite system. He was also organizing various studies on the economics of supersonic air transport and of satellite navigation. He served as chairman of the Interagency Committee on Atmospheric Science, as representative on the Federal Council for Science and Technology, as consultant to the President's Science Advisory Committee, and as the Department of Commerce repre-

[7] Ralph M. Hower and Charles D. Orth, *Managers and Scientists* (Cambridge: Harvard University Press, 1963), p. 240.

[8] Subcommittee on Deficiencies of the Committee on Appropriations, House of Representatives, 87th Congress, Second Session, *Hearings on Supplemental Appropriations Bill*, August 1962, p. 34.

sentative to the Federal Radiation Council. According to Hollomon's own estimate, the CITP took up only about fifteen per cent of his time.

Hollomon's personal style had great impact, and in fact had a great deal to do with the way the CITP case developed. He has been variously described as a "bright, peppery young man," [9] "a dissatisfied person . . . an inventor, and innovator," [10] an "enfant terrible —he knew how to get things done; I still have the scars," "abrasive," "a man in a hurry," "politically inept," "aggressive," and "persuasive." [11] In a study of technical administrators, one "Dr. Dartell"—understood to be a pseudonym for Hollomon—has been described as follows: "His lively interest and his strong identification with his subject made it easier for the observers to accept what they would otherwise have regarded as a somewhat blunt and almost abrasive personality." [12] From the record of the congressional hearings on the CITP, he appears outspoken, very direct, intensely involved, impatient with the plodding pace of political procedure, and not inclined to approach a problem discreetly and with political circumspection or finesse. He plunged into the political arena with confidence, purpose, and energy, and some disdain for both the congressional committee and the construction industry; he

[9] David Allison, "The Civilian Technology Lag," *International Science and Technology*, 24, December 1963, pp. 24–34.

[10] National Science Foundation, *Technology Transfer and Innovation* (NSF 67–5, 1966), p. 32.

[11] Personal interviews. [12] Hower and Orth, *op. cit.*, p. 239.

was equipped with vigorous arguments to which he confidently anticipated a substantive response. His energy and argumentation proved to be an insufficient substitute for carefully worked out strategies, however, and his own sense of urgency concerning the program contributed to its defeat.

The Program: Its Introduction and Reception in Congress

Research is the business world's equivalent of motherhood. . . . History does not record the name of the last businessman to stand up and publicly denounce research; perhaps it happened before the invention of writing. A few people, however, think that there is an outside chance of this event being repeated.[13]

Just two months after his appointment to the Department of Commerce, Hollomon plunged into the task of persuading Congress that the federal government should concern itself with what he saw as the serious inadequacy of segments of American private industry, and proposed the CITP as an effort in this direction.[14] The CITP was to be an independent agency within the Department of Commerce, "designed first to encourage research and development activities in geographical areas not now attracting scientists and engineers, in research

---

[13] *The Constructor*, August 1963.

[14] The CITP was prepared for presentation to Congress with the assistance of Robert Stern, a special assistant to Hollomon from September 1962 to June 1964, and later with the assistance of John Eberhard, who came on the scene in June 1963.

fields that are oriented toward the civilian sector of the economy, and in industries that are technologically lagging; and second, to make the information resulting from government-sponsored research and development more immediately available and useful to private industry." [15]

With respect to the construction industry, the CITP would encourage building science and technology centers in colleges and universities; award building research and development contracts for developing new materials, building components, and concepts of building technology; develop and refine the modular concept; collect data to guide construction and land development; and study the probable course and impact of future technological development. As Hollomon described it at the time, "The approach will be a systems one with the structure considered as a whole rather than by segment. Moreover, the study will be unfettered by existing practices, codes and regulations; it will seek to determine the ideal shelter for man's needs. . . . It will assess the capability of present technology to provide that ideal shelter and indicate what technical developments in the future are needed and possible to achieve that goal." [16] (See Appendix I.) Finally, the CITP would disseminate information on building science and technology.

The organization of the CITP differed from that of the program proposed by BRAB. Hollomon intended an independent agency which would contract research and development to other agencies, such as the NBS and

[15] Subcommittee on Deficiencies, 87th Congress, *op. cit.*, p. 45.
[16] *Ibid.*, p. 49.

various research institutes. Seeking major change in bureaucratic responsiveness to the problems of civilian technology, he considered the main advantage of the CITP to lie in its independence of existing bureaus. On this he ran into conflict with the objectives of the NBS, which had contracted the Folsom (BRAB) study in order to develop its own building research program within the bureau. The preference of Allan Astin, director of the NBS, and Allan Bates of the Building Research Division of the NBS was to implement the Folsom report, and they did not take an active part in the planning of the CITP or in the political activities involved in seeking appropriations.

The initial budget proposal for the CITP was regarded as developmental; the intention, according to Hollomon, was to build a $50-million program.[17] The design of the proposal was based on the recommendations of the White House Panel and the discussions and documents described above. According to Hollomon the main stimulus was the Galbraith-Wiesner memorandum. The proposal was supported by Luther Hodges, secretary of commerce, and cleared by the Bureau of the Budget, which had been involved in planning sessions. However, the bureau recommended that for strategic purposes Hollomon seek special legislative support to buttress his request to the Appropriations Committee. But Hollomon

---

[17] Opponents of the program claim that Hollomon intended to build a $14-billion program—essentially taking over the building industry (personal communications, Douglas Whitlock).

chose to rely on the very broad authority under which the Department of Commerce operated: the Commerce Clearing-House Act of 1950, through which the department may provide technical information service for industry; a research grant law of 1958; and a provision under which the department has authority to foster, promote, and develop commerce, manufacturing, and shipping industries of the United States. In retrospect, the advice to establish legislative underpinnings was sound, and Hollomon was later to follow it in seeking appropriations for other programs, such as the State Technical Services Program of 1965. But in 1961, with little political experience and minimal guidance, he disregarded the advice.

Hollomon made a number of important changes in his proposal during the year in which he was requesting congressional appropriations for the program, as can be seen in Table 6. Note that in February 1963 the House limited its appropriations to the textile research component of the proposal and that Hollomon chose not to request restoration of the building-research component. Later, when the Senate supported the House recommendations, the CITP was dropped by the Department of Commerce as an independent bureau, and in June 1964 the fragments of the program were formally incorporated into the National Bureau of Standards.

The process by which the building-research part of the CITP was aborted—and the entire proposal essentially rejected—was a complex one, affected by the mode in which it was presented, congressional relationships at

Table 6. CIIP appropriations requests

Date	Hearings	Estimated requirement	Program	Amount appropriated
August 1962	House of Representatives Subcommittee on Deficiencies of Committee on Appropriations *	$3,800,000 (Fiscal year 1963)	$ 1.6m–textile research 1.0m–building research 450,000–study of other industries 450,000–Industrial Technical Services 300,000–administration	None
March 1963	Revised request to Subcommittee on Deficiencies	1,250,000 (Fiscal year 1963)	500,000–textile research 300,000–building research 164,000–study of other industries 200,000–Industrial Technical Services 86,000–administration	$625,000
February 1963	House of Representatives Subcommittee on Appropriations for the Departments of State, Justice and Commerce *	7,400,000 (Fiscal year 1964)	2.0m †–textile research 1.6m †–building research 1.6m †–other industries 1.7m–University-Industry Technical Service 500,000–administration	$1.0m for textiles program only
October 1963	Senate Subcommittee on Appropriations for the Departments of State, Justice and Commerce.	4,700,000 restoration (Fiscal year 1964)	1.0m–textile research 1.6m–other industries 1.7m–University-Industry Technical Service 400,000–administration	No restoration; $1.0m appropriation of House accepted

* Appendix II for list of committee members.
† Not formally broken down—Hollomon's estimates at hearings.

the time, and a number of political factors which had little to do directly with the program itself, but which nevertheless had a bearing on its reception by the Appropriations Committee.

Three kinds of objections were raised in the hearings: procedural, ideological and substantive, and they were closely intertwined in the arguments of the program's opponents.

I want to call the immediate attention of the Congress to a clumsy and highly suspect attempt by a major federal agency to undertake on behalf of the vast United States construction industry, and without its invitation, participation or guidance, an ill-conceived and ill-defined research program that would tamper with the delicate free enterprise mechanisms of the highly competitive $80 billion per year industry, undercut that industry's own substantial research and development efforts, create a costly and self-perpetuating program that offers little prospect of benefit, set up a new era of political patronage, and would introduce to the American taxpayer a new brand of government bureaucrat, the technocrat.[18]

The procedural objection to the "clumsy and highly suspect attempt" hinged on the presentation of the proposal as a deficiency item, rather than as an item for the regular hearings of the Subcommittee on Appropriations for the Department of Commerce, to be held in early 1963. The Subcommittee on Deficiencies Appropriations

[18] Address by Congressman Frank Bow to House of Representatives on February 21, 1963, *Congressional Record*, vol. 109, pt. 2 (Washington, D.C.: GPO), p. 2754.

was established in 1959 as a move to cut down on supplementary requests by channeling them all into a single subcommittee. The ambiguity in the definition of the responsibilities of this subcommittee [19] became apparent in the CITP situation. The subcommittee usually functions as a channel for emergency requests to supplement an existing appropriation. The CITP budget request was unusual in that it was intended to fund a new project. Hollomon justified his request by citing the urgency evident in the statements and documents from the Office of the President. He argued that there was an immediate need to match the current growth of the space and defense sectors with a similar growth in the civilian sector. He also argued that his appointment had been recent, indeed subsequent to the meeting of the regular Appropriations Subcommittee for 1963.

Hollomon was clearly in a hurry. Following the regular appropriations hearings for fiscal year 1964, he was to resubmit his request for supplemental appropriations—this time in order to get the program initiated immediately, instead of waiting a few months for the regular bill to be considered.

That others in the department approved the unusual strategy of using the Deficiencies Subcommittee reflected a desire to get the program underway prior to going to the regular Subcommittee on Appropriations, which historically had not been favorably disposed to the Department of Commerce. John Rooney (Democrat/New

[19] Richard F. Fenno, *The Power of the Purse* (Boston: Little Brown, 1966), p. 239.

York), chairman of the regular Appropriations Sub-committee, is a formidable obstacle, generally wary of new programs, particularly those in the Department of Commerce. He is, in fact, reputed to favor programs only within the FBI and the Maritime Administration. In proposing the CITP, it was advantageous to try to circumvent Rooney. Although he was also a member of the Deficiencies Subcommittee, there he was in a less powerful position. But Hollomon did, in any case, clash with Rooney, who was clearly not about to rush into supporting a new program. Rooney's antagonism was such that, in 1965, during the hearings for the State Technical Services Program, he was to order an FBI investigation of Hollomon, accusing him of lobbying for the Department of Commerce.

Hollomon's strategy backfired. Both Rooney and Frank Bow (Republican/Ohio), a member of the Rooney Committee and the Deficiencies Subcommittee, made explicit their opposition. "I object to this program being handled as a deficiency item. The regular committee has had hearings in this connection with next year's bill and I think this should be referred to them since this is a new item." [20]

However, the chairman of the Deficiencies Subcommittee, Albert Thomas (Democrat/Texas) seemed at first favorably disposed toward the program, and Hollo-

---

[20] Subcommittee on Deficiencies of the Committee on Appropriations, House of Representatives, 88th Congress, 1st Session, *Hearings on Supplemental Appropriations Bill* (March 1963), p. 137.

mon's approach might have worked had not action on all the deficiencies appropriations during the end of fiscal year 1962 been delayed for reasons which had nothing directly to do with the CITP. On October 12, 1962, Clarence Cannon (Democrat/Missouri), chairman of the Appropriations Committee, postponed all final action on the Supplementary Appropriations Bill for fiscal 1963, stating that he wanted to hold down federal spending and that there was nothing of immediate urgency which could not be held over until 1963.[21] This was a move to deal with a procedural question concerning the Senate's right to add to House-passed appropriations. It had particular bearing on the CITP case, since postponement of the decision on the supplemental appropriations allowed Rooney to reinforce his opposition to the program.

The ideological objections to the CITP were raised immediately in the first hearing of the Subcommittee on Deficiencies. Bow picked up Hollomon's statement that "it is of the utmost importance to the well being of the nation that these valuable [R&D] resources be allocated carefully among those areas where our need is the greatest," [22] and interpreted it as a "line out of an ideology." Bow's position concerning the implications of allocating federal funds to the private sector "according to need" and possibly upsetting the "delicate free enterprise mechanism," dominated the mood of the subsequent hearings. Later, Bow expressed his concern that government would

[21] *Congressional Quarterly*, October 19, 1962.
[22] Subcommittee on Deficiencies, 87th Congress, *op. cit.*, p. 46.

penalize the efficient producer, and thus impair the existing R&D effort in private industry: "And the [firm] who does not use its own funds and set up its own research, you will do that for him, so in that way you are helping the less efficient give competition to the fellow doing it for himself?" [23]

Bow was the first to express this kind of objection; other congressmen were to follow. In the 1962 hearings, Representative Thomas indicated some enthusiasm for the proposal as one which could stimulate private research. In February 1963, however, he questioned Hollomon as follows: "One would come to the conclusion from what you say that what has been going on in the last ten to fifteen years has been to the embarrassment and chagrin of private industry and it has been caused by government, and that is not an accurate picture. You do not want government to go to private industry and tell them to hire scientists? . . . And now you want government to appropriate money to urge industry to do what you think the government should have been telling them to do the last fifteen years? . . . We do not want government in business and here you are doing just that." [24]

At one point Hollomon tried to counter the argument in the same terms: "The rate of growth of the Soviet economy gives force to Khrushchev's threat that the so-

[23] Subcommittee for Departments of State, Justice and Commerce of the Committee on Appropriations, House of Reppresentatives, 88th Congress, First Session, *Hearings* (Washington, D.C.: GPO, 1964), p. 794.

[24] Subcommittee on Deficiencies, 88th Congress, *op. cit.*, p. 127.

cialist state will defeat the United States on the economic battlefield." [25] But he made explicit, particularly after the first round of criticism in August 1962, that his intention was not to support individual firms, but was "to provide to all the firms technical information which would permit all of them to become more effective, more productive." [26] To meet the ideological objections, in fact, Hollomon changed the proposal significantly; but the original skepticism persisted, and bolstered several other objections relating to the content of the proposal.

The most vigorous of the objections to substance was that there was already a great deal of research being carried out within the industry, but that due to the competitive nature of the industry, much of the research by individual firms was not public. Industry, it was argued, has its own mechanisms for managing and coordinating research independent of federal activity. It was contended that the CITP would have no unique function, but would duplicate the activities of other agencies which operated to disseminate technical ideas, to develop criteria for building standards, and to encourage innovation in construction. For example, John Rooney claimed that the CITP would duplicate the existing National Bureau of Standards activities in disseminating technical information to industry.

Hollomon maintained that the overlap was in fact minimal since the NBS was not permitted to act as a

[25] Subcommittee for Departments of State, Justice and Commerce, *Hearings, op. cit.*, p. 765.

[26] *Ibid.*, p. 794.

contract-letting agency; and further, he planned to transfer some CITP appropriations to the bureau. This, however, remained a sensitive issue within the Department of Commerce and the substantive question of overlapping functions of federal agencies remained a predominant theme of the controversy.

Finally, it was argued that the program might impose a strain on the federal budget, adding a responsibility that should be borne by the private sector. Underlying these objections was the contention by congressmen that the CITP proposal did not represent the view of the industry, that none of the 110 trade and professional associations in the construction industry had been consulted by the Department of Commerce when it formulated the CITP.

It soon became clear that the congressional reception to the construction industry component was jeopardizing the entire CITP and Hollomon abandoned it. Yet the Appropriations Committee remained apprehensive that some of the rejected provisions would be "buried" within other programs in the NBS. In later hearings, Rooney commented to Allan Astin who was proposing expansion of the NBS, "Isn't it strange Doctor, that these are the very items turned down by Congress last year? . . . Is an attempt being made to bury the unpopular programs thought up by Dr. Hollomon which aroused the American people to such an extent that we were flooded with mail last year and threatened if we appropriated 15¢ for some of the items in the project?" [27]

[27] Subcommittee for Departments of State, Justice and Commerce, *Hearings*, Part 5, February 21, 1964, p. 633.

III / *Opposition and Support*

Congressional Opposition

The negative reception in Congress to the CITP is to be understood both in terms of the varying styles of representation among committee members and of the mood of Congress with respect to presidential spending programs. Congress in the early 1960's was divided and reluctant to move ahead with new programs. The slim margin by which John F. Kennedy had won the presidential election in 1960 indicated a slight shift in voter attitudes; but this was not similarly reflected in Congress. The activities of the 87th and 88th Congress have been described as reflecting "a hardening congressional position toward Administration-sponsored measures, especially those involving spending."[1] This "hardening position" only reinforced the usual congressional fastidiousness about executive-sponsored domestic spending."[2]

[1] Frederic N. Cleaveland et al., *Congress and Urban Problems* (Washington, D.C.: Brookings Institution, 1969), p. 12.

[2] The legislative record for the approval of presidential proposals submitted to Congress was generally from about 40% to 50% approval at that time. In 1962 the Congress granted only

The litany was to "protect the Budget." Protecting the budget was, after all, the formal concern of the Appropriations Committee. Historically mistrustful of the Bureau of the Budget as an adequate guardian of the Treasury,[3] Congress was little influenced by the bureau support of the CITP. "I feel there is too much money already in this Office of Technology in the Department of Commerce. They have so much time that they can cause about a thousand people to descend upon us by telephone, correspondence, and by other means, to try and get their money from the taxpayers' U.S. Treasury." [4]

Budget cutting was encouraged by Kennedy who, while urging new domestic programs to bolster the civilian economy, also emphasized the budgetary problems

---

44.3% of Kennedy's specific legislative proposals. But comparison with Eisenhower's record is difficult, since Kennedy asked for much more.

Year	Proposals submitted	Proposals approved	Per cent approved
1958	234	110	47.0
1959	228	93	40.8
1960	183	56	30.6
1961	355	172	48.4
1962	298	132	44.3

The figures are from the *Congressional Quarterly*, November 23, 1962, pp. 2187–2190.

[3] Fenno, *op. cit.*, p. 101.

[4] Statement by John Rooney, Subcommittee for Departments of State, Justice and Commerce of the Committee on Appropriations, *Hearings, op. cit.*, 1963, p. 1538.

facing the government. His 1962 *Budget Message to Congress* began by noting that "because of the increasing requirements for national security, I have applied strict standards of urgency in reviewing proposed expenditure in this budget. Many desirable new products and activities are being deferred." [5] The Appropriations Committee was quick to point out that Kennedy's concern for new domestic programs was inconsistent with such deferrals.

Perhaps the most vivid indication of congressional intransigence during 1962 and 1963 was the snail's pace of appropriation bills, particularly those related to domestic urban programs. The administration sponsored numerous urban problem-oriented bills: "The agenda of every congressional session . . . was filled with domestic and economic aid questions, revolving around proposals for area redevelopment . . . housing and urban renewal, federal aid to education and grants-in-aid programs . . . and the like." [6] Many were rejected by Congress. One, for example, was a bill sponsored by President Kennedy and widely supported by liberal labor lobbies and the nation's mayors, planners, and architects to establish a Cabinet-level Department of Urban Affairs. This, like the CITP, was strongly opposed by the building industry on the grounds of federal infringement on the private sector. Here, as in the

[5] President John F. Kennedy *Budget Message to Congress,* January 18, 1962.

[6] Cleaveland, *op. cit.,* p. 12.

CITP case, the Chamber of Commerce opposed the extension of federal activities as "socialistic," a step down the "primrose path of centralism," and an unwarranted concentration of power in the federal government.[7]

It was not until after Kennedy's assassination on November 22, 1963, that the opposition to federal activity eased, and this was reflected in the changing urban-development policy with increased centralized planning, culminating in the Housing and Urban Development (HUD) Act of 1965. But the CITP went before the 88th Congress prior to the assassination when the mood was one of annoyance at the quantity of domestic issues and of reluctance to proliferate Executive-level programs. "The role of committees, their chairmen, and often their anti-administration majority was thus found to be one of obstruction—and sometimes destruction . . . of major administration legislation."[8]

The problems caused by the congressional mood with respect to federal spending were compounded by the orientation of the major congressional actors in the CITP case. It is useful to consider an analysis that characterizes representatives in terms of the "roles" they play.[9] A representative can assume the role of "trustee," following his own conscience and inclinations. This may

[7] *Ibid.*, p. 11.

[8] *Congressional Quarterly*, November 23, 1962, p. 196.

[9] Heinz Eulau et al., "The Role of the Representative," *American Political Science Review*, 53, 3, September 1, 1959, pp. 742ff.

be the situation when a representative's constituency is so diverse as to leave him a great deal of freedom, when the issues may be of little interest to his constituency, or when his position is so secure that he has freedom to follow his own inclinations. John Rooney and Albert Thomas appear to fit this role. On the other hand, Frank Bow seemed to play the role of a "delegate," a representative subject to the pressures of a particular group within his constituency. A brief history of each of these congressional participants illuminates how their style of representation affected their response to the CITP proposal.

John Rooney was an assistant district attorney in Brooklyn before going to Washington. He was reputed to be hard working and cautious, with a tendency to focus on the picayune, and to be a biting cross-examiner who had adopted the philosophy that those who request appropriations are "guilty unless proven otherwise." On his staff were former members of the FBI, an agency he is reputed to favor. He has been described [10] as "a balding, undersized Uncle Sam with bad digestion," as "the great needler from Brooklyn" and, by James Reston, as "one of the most powerful men in America in a negative way." He has also been described as a congressman's congressman: "the Congress knows that when the gentleman from New York, congressman Rooney, handles the Committee bill on the floor, that the previous work

[10] Peter Wyden, "The Man Who Frightens Bureaucrats," *Saturday Evening Post*, January 31, 1959, pp. 27ff.

of the Committee . . . [has] culled out and eliminated within human error every major objection to its enactment." [11]

Rooney is the epitome of the "trustee" representative. With a highly diverse Brooklyn constituency, he could comfortably indulge his single-minded inclination to save money. "I approach [the budget] with the idea that it can be cut." He is particularly concerned with those new research programs likely to expand. "This may be only $250 but this is like the camel's nose, these things never get out of the budget, they manage to stay and grow." [12]

Historically, this has indeed been true—that research ultimately leads to active and expensive programs. The pattern of large-scale federal programs in agriculture is a case in point; for it began with the early scientific interest in fostering the development and application of technical improvements relevant to agriculture. "Research was influential, not merely because the politicians were persuaded by effective data; an even more important reason may have been that scientists . . . were the major organized communities of professional opinion with a continuous interest in specific public programs." [13]

Rooney was also concerned about what he regarded as a waste of research funds suggested by the form of

[11] Roland Libonati in *Congressional Record*, September 14, 1962, p. 19514.

[12] Aaron Wildavsky, *The Politics of the Budgetary Process* (Boston: Little Brown, 1964), pp. 48, 112.

[13] Don K. Price, *The Scientific Estate* (Cambridge: Harvard University Press, 1965), p. 63.

the CITP proposal. He queried Hollomon: "You are in effect asking for a blank check are you not?" [14] Rooney spoke disparagingly of government officials, particularly those with new "imaginative" projects; he referred to Luther Hodges, secretary of the Department of Commerce, as "Mr. Hodge-Podge." Although Hollomon had never himself confronted John Rooney prior to the CITP hearings, his association with Hodges, and past confrontations between his department and Rooney contributed to the tenor of Rooney's opposition to the CITP.

In addition, Rooney played on the strains of the Department, taunting Hollomon for taking on NBS functions. At later hearings he was to taunt Astin, the director of the NBS: "Dr. Astin used to run this show. Now he has a new boss, Dr. Hollomon." [15]

The late Representative Albert Thomas from Texas, chairman of the Deficiencies Subcommittee, had long been concerned with overlapping federal programs and federal spending, and had most notably demonstrated this concern with respect to housing proposals. The Thomas Amendment to the Housing Bill of 1959 had been an attempt to prevent "backdoor" spending; that is, the financing of federal programs that avoided the economy-minded Appropriations Committee. Thomas was favorably disposed toward the CITP during the

[14] Subcommittee for the Department of State, Justice, and Commerce of the Committee on Appropriations, *op. cit.*, 1963, p. 773.

[15] *Ibid.*, February 21, 1964, p. 633.

first hearings; but later he observed that the Housing and Home Finance Agency had for twelve years concerned itself with developing and establishing criteria for the evaluation of new building materials. Hollomon replied to Thomas that he intended a working relationship between the CITP and the HHFA. He might also have noted that in 1960 the HHFA spent only $15,000 on housing research; less, in fact, than the Department of Agriculture spent on chicken coops.[16]

The most outspoken opponent of the program was Congressman Bow, who called it "the most ill-conceived, amateurish and dangerous proposal that I have seen in many years."[17] And "as close to destruction of the free enterprise system as anything can get."[18] Bow was known as the chairman of the Bow Task Force, a special subcommittee of Republicans formally organized in February 1963 "to conduct a detailed line by line survey of the budget and make recommendations as to where savings could be made."[19] These savings included "a considerable portion" of civilian and military new non-emergency construction. The Task Force also urged a moratorium on all new programs.[20] Hiring its own staff and formulating its own targets for budget reductions,

[16] Martin Meyerson, Barbara Perrett, and William Wheaton, *Housing, People, and Cities* (New York: McGraw-Hill, 1962), p. 340.
[17] Bernard Spring, "Research for Building: The Big Battle Rages in Washington," *Architectural Forum*, 119, 2 (September 1963), 123.
[18] *The Washington Post*, Saturday, July 6, 1963.
[19] *Congressional Record*, March 4, 1963, p. 3236.
[20] This was discussed at a March 4 meeting (*Congressional Quarterly*, March 15, 1963, p. 326).

the Task Force was essentially a product of partisan politics and violated the nonpartisan norms of the House Committee on Appropriations.

The strength and character of Bow's opposition to the CITP can in part be explained in terms of his home constituency. The state of Ohio ranks first in the nation in the number of employees in the stone, clay, and glass products industries, and these industries are concentrated in the eastern part of the state, primarily within Bow's district.[21] The major source of employment in Stark County, within his district, is ceramic wall and floor tiles. These industries, concerned about public control of technological innovation in materials development, took an active position against the CITP. They were threatened by the possible development of competitive materials as a result of a government R&D program. Since the installation of bricks and tiles is labor-intensive, innovative materials requiring less labor would pose a significant threat.

The clay industries were represented most actively by Douglas Whitlock, founder of the Structural Clay Products Institute, the national trade association of a $260-million industry, eleven of whose member companies and contributing associates were from the state of Ohio. Whitlock was a personal friend of Frank Bow, having worked for many years with him in Republican politics.

The opposition of Bow, the "delegate" representative of this constituency, reinforced Rooney's passion to avoid spending. Despite the considerable support for

[21] State of Ohio Department of Industrial and Economic Development, *Ohio Manufacturing* (1962).

the CITP from the White House, those opposing the program continued to dominate the hearings.

Public Opposition

What ultimately killed the building-industry component of the CITP was the political power of the construction industry, the strength and tenacity of which was not fully appreciated by Hollomon. As has been noted above (pp. 5–14), while the technological state of the industry had potential adverse consequences for growing housing needs, the industry was by no means facing an economic crisis. Moreover, the very fragmentation that impeded technological change within the industry gave it a broad political base. Vocal public reaction against the program provided political support for the congressional opposition. For example, at the Senate hearings on October 22, 1963, Senator John L. McClellan (Democrat/Arkansas) itemized the communications he had received from the public concerning the CITP. Fourteen communications were in favor of the program and requested the Senate to increase the $1 million appropriated by the House. McClellan also received sixty-four communications opposed to the program,[22] almost all of them from the construction industry or related organizations.

The building industry had an organized political base in the Construction and Community Development De-

[22] Communications in favor of the CITP were distributed as follows: three from universities, five from industrial research organizations, one from a bank, three from industry, two from professional associations. Of the communications opposed to the

partment of the Chamber of Commerce. Douglas Whitlock was the spokesman for the Chamber of Commerce and worked closely with James F. Steiner, the manager and secretary of the Construction and Community Development Department. The chamber conducted a survey in February 1963 of 110 trade and professional associations in the building industry, which found that none of those organizations had been consulted by Hollomon in formulating the CITP. The Chamber of Commerce argued that the only meetings held with construction industry representatives had been for the purpose of enlisting support for a plan already developed.

Representing the industry, the Chamber of Commerce distributed, on May 31, 1963, a special report, written by James Steiner and addressed to construction-industry leaders. It called for immediate action opposing the CITP as an instance of federal intervention in the activities of the construction industry. The report leveled several arguments against the CITP. It denied that the construction industry was a "lagging" industry, asserting that it was, indeed, conducting research, and that there was no evidence in any of the government reports to support a contrary view.

The report said that neither the BRAB report, the White House Panel findings, nor the CITP had been based on a study of the existing R&D in the construction industry. Thus, "the program for scientific research

---

program, at least thirty-eight were clearly from the building industry. Seven were from building associations or institutes, and two were from engineering firms. Seventeen were from individuals with no stated institutional affiliation.

begins from an unscientific basis." [23] It argued that the documents cited by Hollomon as supportive did not support his plan and, further, that the scope and purpose of the CITP had been changed from an initial concern with "building research" to a federally subsidized program for the entire construction industry. Discrepancies were noted between Hollomon's promise not to support development of proprietary products and his plan to make research available to firms that did not have a broad enough spectrum of products or services to carry on an independent R&D program. There was concern, reiterated by Rooney in the hearings, that the program was seeking a "blank check," that its projected use of funds was unclear. Finally, the Chamber of Commerce report claimed that the Building Research Institute (BRI) would be weakened by the CITP, as would the research activities of private enterprise.

The BRI was founded by the National Academy of Sciences, National Research Council, and incorporated in 1962 as an independent technical society, "a focal point for the stimulation and conduct of needed research and development in the building industry on the broadest possible scale." [24] But with a $150,000-a-year budget, the

[23] Construction and Community Development Department, Chamber of Commerce of the United States, *Federal Subsidies for Research and Development in the Construction Industry. Special Report for Construction Industry Leaders* (Chamber of Commerce, May 31, 1963).

[24] Building Research Institute, news release, November 1, 1963. The BRI, with headquarters in Washington, represents various segments of the construction industry. Its objective is to promote the "advancement of every aspect of the science

activity of the BRI had not gone far beyond the collection and dissemination of information.[25]

Despite this record, the Chamber of Commerce turned to the Building Research Institute as an agency to coordinate research independent of government activity. It was argued that the federal intervention that BRAB considered necessary would, contrary to its intentions, slow down economic growth. "If the federal government takes the responsibility for R&D in the construction industry . . . then the industry must wait for government decisions before making efforts towards innovation through its business firms and associations." [26]

The Chamber of Commerce report urged members to attend the National Construction Industry Research and Development Conference in October to discuss R&D activities in the construction industry. This conference was held on October 17–18, 1963, in Washington, and one of the invited speakers was Herbert Hollomon, who talked about the economic importance of science and technology. Two hundred and eighty representatives of building materials and trade associations, architects, and contractors attended. One of the most active participants

---

of building and buildings, the systems and services in all the arts, technologies and practices it comprises, through the collaboration of individuals and organizations in all sectors of the industries and professions associated with building, to the end that better building and buildings will be provided for the general welfare of mankind."

[25] Building Research Institute, *Building Science News*, August 1962.

[26] Construction and Community Development Department, *op. cit.*

was Douglas Whitlock, who had probably the most influence as an individual on the decision of the Appropriations Subcommittee,[27] through his success in articulating the traditional concerns of much of the building industry about government intervention.

Whitlock had, as we have seen, many ties to the building industry as an officer in the Building Products Institute, the Structural Clay Products Institute, and the Producers' Council. He has been an active member of the Republican party since his student days, when he founded the first Young Republicans Club in the United States at the University of Indiana. Whitlock was an important behind-the-scenes figure in Republican party activities. During several campaigns he was a member of the presidential campaign staff, directing tour arrangements for Goldwater, Eisenhower, and Nixon.[28]

Concerned with government intervention in private industry, Whitlock had long tried to keep the federal government out of R&D activities related to the building industry. His opposition to the CITP was a continuation of a history of behind-the-scenes activities with respect to new federal proposals—activities which had been effective in preventing federal appropriations in the area of building technology. With the support of many others in the construction industry, he was especially concerned with research bearing on building products. Government development of new materials, he believed,

27 *Science,* 140, June 28, 1963, p. 1380, and Bernard Spring, *op. cit.*

28 *Congressional Quarterly,* September 25, 1964, p. 2223.

would interfere with the competitive balance in the industry. "The Program would have the effect of shifting dependence for Research and Development to federal subsidized programs and away from private construction industry firms and associations. . . . [This] would result in the selection of one part of the industry to which to give special research effort and by doing so, would upset the competitive balance of industry segments."[29]

The CITP was concerned with the building industry as only one of several industries that underutilized technology. Whitlock, however, saw the program as focused on the building industry, and he anticipated a massive program of government intervention. He claimed that Hollomon had included the textile industry in the program as a token to Luther Hodges, and that the intention was to develop a $14-billion government program essentially to take over all building-industry research.

In May 1963, Whitlock testified at the CITP hearings on behalf of the Chamber of Commerce.[30] Familiar with congressional prejudices of the time, he played his role well, focusing on issues of federal paternalism, threats to free enterprise, the waste of government money, and the empire building implied in the activities of the federal government. He presented the Chamber of Commerce objections to the CITP, emphasizing that Hollomon had

[29] Douglas Whitlock, testimony, Subcommittee on Appropriations, *op. cit.*, p. 1537.

[30] Subcommittee for the Departments of State, Justice and Commerce of the Committee on Appropriations, *op. cit.*, p. 1535.

neglected to consult the leadership organizations in the construction industry. And he insisted there was already a building-research program in the industry, though it was somewhat hidden owing to competitive relationships that led to secrecy on matters of innovation.

In view of his perspective on the implications of government activity, Whitlock regarded the Folsom (BRAB) report as a "sellout." He was highly critical of BRAB, claiming it had weakened considerably, that its members were poorly informed about the actual state of research, and that the conclusions of the report were not supported by industry. Interestingly, it was one of the authors of the BRAB report, William H. Scheick who had first encouraged Whitlock to become involved in opposing Hollomon.

Scheick was executive director of the American Institute of Architects (AIA), and in 1949 he had been hand-picked by Douglas Whitlock to be the first director of BRAB. Scheick's opposition to the CITP was revealed rather suddenly during the full hearings before the regular Subcommittee on Appropriations in February 1963.

In preparation for these hearings, Hollomon called a meeting of representatives from universities and professional associations on January 18, 1963, to discuss which areas of educational and technical activity in the building industry could be effectively stimulated by federal support. Participants included members of BRAB, the American Institute of Architects (AIA), and the American Society of Civil Engineers (ASCE). The discussion indicated that the group was sympathetic to the plan of the CITP. In view of this, Hollomon must have been discouraged in the February 1963 hearings when Rooney presented him with a letter from Scheick stating that "we are absolutely opposed to the use of federal government funds for any support by matching funds or otherwise of research programs or projects connected with the innovation or development of building materials or products by industry trade associations or individual firms." [31] He opposed government support for product innovation or any activity that might be identified with particular firms or products, and cited a cement-industry representative who had argued that "if we sponsor research for basementless slabs, we don't get the concrete that goes into the foundation."

Scheick was writing in his capacity as director of the AIA, but his reservations about the CITP reflected those of BRAB as well. These were aired in response to a letter in February 1963 from Bow to Frederick Seitz, the president of the National Academy of Sciences. In the letter Bow asked if Hollomon's program was consistent with the BRAB report recommendations. Seitz had Richard H. Tatlow, the chairman of BRAB, reply to Bow. Hollomon saw Tatlow's letter for the first time when Bow presented it at the February hearings. With devastating simplicity the letter explained that the two proposals did "appear to differ in their objectives, and could therefore differ in significant details." [32] Tatlow emphasized that the BRAB proposal had been limited to

[31] The letter, dated February 1, 1963, appears in Subcommittee of the Committee on Appropriations, *op. cit.*, pp. 1151–1152. Scheick was also a member of BRAB and the BRI.

[32] *Ibid.*, p. 780.

changes within the National Bureau of Standards, to strengthen their building-research activities. He concluded that there was no need for government to concern itself with industrial product or process innovation.

Immediately after the February hearings, Hollomon set up one meeting with BRAB, and another with forty building-industry representatives. On the basis of these discussions he altered his proposal, restating it in a form similar to the BRAB report. The restatement stressed that government support would not be provided for product development. It excluded the plan to award contracts to develop new products and building components, and focused on four points: (1) development of a continuing census of public and private building and construction research and technical activity; (2) collection, collation, and dissemination of nonproprietary building information covering design, construction, operations, maintenance, and performance; (3) development of physical-performance criteria and measurement and testing methods for materials, components, structures, and structure environments; and (4) development of "fundamental knowledge" on environmental requirement for people in relation to buildings, building design and behavior in relation to man and the forces of nature, and processes of building design, construction, operations, maintenance and retirement. At this time Hollomon asked the National Academy of Sciences to recommend an advisory board to the CITP. Fourteen men were appointed, including the president of the AFL-CIO Building and Construction Trades Department, and

Robert B. Taylor, director of the Structural Clay Products Research Foundation. Five members were from BRAB (see Appendix III).

The revision of the proposal won support from BRAB, from the AIA, and from several professional engineering associations. These associations were in a very awkward position with respect to the CITP. On the one hand, their clients—the builders—were opposed to the program; on the other, the associations were supposed to be the progressive force in the industry. Their dilemma was reflected in their vacillation. The AIA, for example, opposed the program in February 1963, but when their position was criticized in an article in the September 1963 *Architectural Forum*,[33] Scheick responded that he did not want to be represented as opposing the CITP. However, the decision to exclude the building-research activities of the CITP had already been made by Hollomon by the time the AIA support was expressed.

A number of engineering associations were either opposed to the CITP or refused to take a position. Most tended to avoid politics, and were neither politically astute nor sensitive even to the many legislative matters that had important bearing on their interests. They were, however, sensitive to the relationship of their members to industry, and tended to take politically safe positions which protected these relationships.

With respect to the CITP, the American Institute of Construction Engineers was opposed to potential gov-

[33] Bernard Spring, *op. cit.*

ernment interference with private enterprise, and argued that they could not support a vaguely-defined program. The American Society of Civil Engineers (ASCE) held an ambiguous position, for they agreed with the original objectives of the program, but not with the proposed administrative format. This position clearly reflected the influence of the ASCE director, Richard Tatlow, who was also at the time chairman of BRAB. Moreover, the ASCE membership overlapped the membership of the Associated General Contractors, a group which openly opposed the CITP.

The ASCE reiterated the BRAB proposal for a National Institute of Building Research tied in with the National Bureau of Standards. William H. Wisely, the executive secretary of the ASCE, doubted the need for a "crash" program. The complicated building-code problem, in his judgment, had first to be resolved. "It is my considered opinion that any approach to Congress for a building research funding program should be deferred until a plan is devised that will have the solid support of *all* segments of the building industry." [34] However, when the building research component was finally taken out of the CITP proposal (prior to the hearings before the Senate Subcommittee on Appropriations), Wisely wrote to Senator McClellan and protested the curtailment of the program. [35]

The National Society of Professional Engineers also

[34] Letter from William H. Wisely to J. Herbert Hollomon, January 21, 1963.

[35] Subcommittee for the Departments of State, Justice and Commerce of the Committee on Appropriations, *op. cit.*, p. 1655.

found it impossible to take an unequivocal stand with respect to the CITP. In the spring of 1963, a poll taken of NSPE membership revealed that the society was split down the middle on the issue of giving support to the CITP. Educators and some small industries supported the program, while larger industrial affiliates and consultants were opposed. The society essentially sidestepped the issue, and in July 1963, stated its position as one favoring a federal "engineering research program" under the policy direction of an engineering-research policy board to develop new technical knowledge for industry.[36] The NSPE opposed research projects for product development or application, and rejected advisory or consulting services to industry. Even when product development was de-emphasized in the CITP, the attitude of the society remained ambivalent.

The potential competition of the CITP in providing consulting services posed an additional problem for the associations. The American Institute of Consulting Engineers supported only the university aspects of the program that would train advanced students, and opposed any arrangement that would bring about university or government competition with private engineering firms.

Considering this response from the engineering community, it is interesting that Hollomon was one of the people instrumental in establishing the National Academy of Engineering in December 1964, as a means of encouraging engineers to apply their skills to social problems.

[36] National Society of Professional Engineers, *Minutes of Annual Meeting* (1963).

The labor unions, potentially interested parties in the case, actually played a minor role. During the early 1960's an important concern of the Building and Construction Trades Department of the AFL-CIO was rising unemployment, which, in January 1963, reached the highest level in fifteen months. Unemployment was in part attributed to new construction methods that were reducing labor needs and in part to the shortage of new building projects. The unions tended to regard innovation in technological processes as threatening.

Very little has been said about automation in the building and construction industry. The truth is, however, we have been affected more severely than any other industry. When one man on each of 20,000 construction jobs is laid off due to a new tool, new method, new material or new equipment, there is no publicity.[37]

The unions were also sensitive to federal government intervention in areas that might affect their membership. In this respect, their interests coincided with those of the industry, and Douglas Whitlock had regular contact with the union about matters of mutual concern. For example, as the keynote speaker at an AFL-CIO conference of apprenticeship directors in January 1963, Whitlock spoke against federal government involvement in apprenticeship programs.

[37] C. J. Haggerty in Bureau of National Affairs, *Construction Labor Report*, 424, November 6, 1963. This concern with the effects of automation culminated in the President's Commission on Technology, Automation and Employment.

Hollomon had predicted union sensitivity to the CITP. He consulted C. J. Haggerty, president of the Building and Construction Trades Department, during the planning of the CITP, and later appointed him to the CITP advisory board. While the unions never supported the program, the contact with Haggerty successfully neutralized the trade union position vis-à-vis the CITP, and there was no union activity, either for or against the program.

Allies of the Program

The CITP did have a few allies, even within the construction industry. One major building group testified strongly in favor of the program—Investing Builders Association (IBA), a trade organization of leading New York City builders, including John Tishman and Harold Uris. The IBA represented 90 per cent of the dollar volume of apartment houses and commercial buildings in New York City. In March 1963, the general manager of Tishman Research Corporation, Joseph Newman, testified before the House Appropriations Committee in support of the CITP and of government activity to unify the building industry, to standardize building codes, and to lessen the lead time between fundamental research and practical applications by "smoothing the road where the profit incentive is lacking or where private enterprise is helpless or indifferent." [38]

[38] Testimony, May 2, 1963, Subcommittee for Departments of State, Justice and Commerce of the Committee on Appropriations, *op. cit.*, 1963, p. 1532.

Support for the CITP also came from several large suppliers—for example, Forest Products, Inc., a Missouri firm which buys lumber and manufactures home building materials. This firm engaged in its own research, but found it difficult to channel its results into the woodworking industry. The owner of the firm likened the situation in construction to that in the postwar agricultural industry, and considered there was pressing need for developing channels of communication between research teams and industry.

Most allies, however, were to be found in educational institutions. Two of the most vocal were Glenn Beyer, director of the Center for Housing and Environmental Studies at Cornell University, and Gordon Fisher, associate dean of engineering at Cornell. Their testimony at the U.S. Senate hearings on April 24, 1963, documented the gap between the current level of research and future housing needs. In addition to their testimony, Beyer and Fisher carried on an extensive correspondence, mainly with professional associations, to gather support for the CITP. At one point Fisher, exasperated by the attitude of Congress toward support of building research, and by its concern with the federal budget, did a small study project on "Peanuts Research." He discovered that the U.S. Department of Agriculture had an unpublicized peanut-research program of substantial dimension, and that there was a bill in Congress at the time to appropriate $1.2 million for a peanut-research laboratory, at an annual operating cost of $750,000. In a letter to Congressman Howard Robison (Republican/New York),

Table 7. Arguments for and against the civilian industrial technology program *

Criticism	Response
The portions of the CITP concerning the building and construction industry are vague and subject to many interpretations.	The CITP followed the line of reasoning in the BRAB report. It was made clear that product development would be excluded, that there would be no in-house research, and that research would be undertaken on a contractual basis by universities and non-profit research groups with no proprietary interests.
The program was developed too fast without adequate time for study.	Except for one aspect, the CITP represents activation of the BRAB report developed over many years, with adequate time for study.
The CITP would result in government domination of the construction industry (and universities).	Regular congressional review of appropriations would prevent such domination of the construction industry; there are precedents in other fields for successful research relationship between government and universities.
The CITP would jeopardize the free enterprise system by destroying and distorting present competitive relationships.	The CITP was not related to proprietary interests, but would benefit entire industry.
The Department of Commerce developed the CITP without properly consulting industry to determine how much is being done and where the federal government fits into the picture.	The construction portion of the CITP was embodied in the BRAB report which, in turn, reflects attitudes strongly held in the construction industry.
Virtually all the construction associations and professional societies oppose this program; industry does not want it.	A large part of the industry is not as well organized as the traditional lobbyist groups within it, and the only means they have to disseminate their views are hearings such as these.
The role of the Building Research Institute has not been given proper attention.	The BRI has not, in fact, been doing any research, and if the legislation is passed, it might well be an agency to participate in CITP.
Industrywide conferences are sufficient for the purpose of stimulating research.	While conferences such as the one sponsored by the U.S. Chamber of Commerce are useful as forums for disseminating information, they do not replace a research program for the industry.

* This is a summary of testimony by Glenn H. Beyer and Gordon P. Fisher to the Senate Subcommittee of the Committee on Appropriations, *Hearings*, 88th Congress, 1st session on H.R. 7063, 1963, pp. 2379–2385.

Fisher wrote: "A lowly peanut seems to have a higher standing than housing or building construction or other things recently defeated in the House Appropriations Bill." [39]

When Hollomon did not request the Senate to restore the construction-research part of the program, Beyer and Fisher wrote a letter, dated November 13, 1963, to Senator Karl Mundt (Republican/South Dakota), a member of the Senate Subcommittee on Appropriations. They asserted that Hollomon was "absolutely wrong" in giving up, and they emphasized the critical social need of such a program. Mundt was urged to restore the funding, despite Hollomon's withdrawal of that part of the program.

The arguments for and against a federal building-research program were reviewed by Beyer and Fisher in their testimony, as they systematically tried to come to grips with the major accusations made by the construction industry. They succinctly summarized the central arguments in the CITP case (see Table 7). But their activities on behalf of the program were used by its opponents as evidence of university eagerness to grab federal funds.

[39] Gordon Fisher, letter to Congressman Howard Robison.

IV / *Technology and the Building Industry*

The process of decision-making with respect to the CITP raises questions concerning the adequacy of the political procedures through which R&D is directed to meet public needs. Only recently has there been a serious national effort to undertake R&D activities to solve urban problems. A major impetus to this effort was the Summer Study on Science and Urban Development at Woods Hole, Massachusetts, in June 1966, sponsored by HUD and the President's Office of Science and Technology. This study brought together ninety-one people from varying backgrounds in government, industry, and universities to discuss applying "the kind of forced draft technological effort that has characterized the development of space and weapons systems . . . to the urban task."[1] Their recommendations formed the basis of HUD's subsequent research efforts.

It has been widely recognized that the success of such

1 Department of Housing and Urban Development, *Science and the City* (Washington, D.C.: GPO, 1967).

an effort hinges not only on technological development, but also on political factors.

Technology never "solves" political problems, or meets public needs, directly. Technical "solutions" are always filtered through the process of politics.[2]

The most difficult question is whether existing or new knowledge and technological processes will be of much use if the objectives for which these should be used cannot be defined clearly through the American political system.[3]

If we are to change our urban environment, we shall need to know not only more about the forces which shape it, but more about the way community decisions are made.[4]

The relationship between technology, politics, and social problems is subtle and complex. Wallace Sayre and Bruce Smith have described a "spectrum of readiness," examining social problems according to the degree to which they are both politically and technologically ready for solution.[5]

With respect to housing, technology is only one of many aspects of the problem. Such factors as land utilization, the cost of and availability of mortgage money,

[2] Wallace S. Sayre and Bruce L. R. Smith, *Government Technology and Social Problems* (Columbia University: Institute for the Study of Science in Human Affairs, 1969), p. 8.

[3] James D. Carroll, "Science and the City: The Question of Authority," *Science*, February 28, 1969, p. 909.

[4] Robert C. Wood, "Science and the City" (reprint, no reference cited).

[5] Sayre and Smith, *op. cit.*

limited market aggregation, and variable consumer taste bear significantly on the extent to which technology is relevant in resolving housing problems. But the salience of political factors, the extent to which the problem of housing is "politically ready" for solution, is of major importance. And much of Hollomon's difficulty in funding the CITP, and, more recently, HUD's difficulties in developing a significant research effort, reflect the importance of political criteria in the process of decision-making about the use of technology.

A number of key issues emerged from this case, in which political, technological, and social factors were all involved. To what extent would the increased use of technology have significant impact on housing? What was the basis of the apparent communications void between the technologists planning the CITP and the congressional opponents to it? What are the character and effect of political and societal constraints on the use of technology for meeting public needs?

For years the building industry had balked at federal proposals to develop R&D programs involving government-industry collaboration. The Public Housing Acts of 1948 and 1949 authorized a government-sponsored research program to study housing codes, technology, and economics. Between 1948 and 1954, Congress appropriated over $5 million for this program; but following industrial opposition, appropriations were suspended in 1953.

The Housing and Home Finance Agency (HHFA) was not funded for research until 1962, at which time only $375,000 was appropriated. Not until the funding, in 1968, of the Housing and Urban Development Department, were substantial appropriations made for urban studies. At this time, appropriations for general urban research were increased from $500,000 to $10 million.[6] This, along with the creation of HUD's office of Urban Technology and Research and the Institute for Urban Development, has added important new dimensions to the urban research picture. A significant effort has been made by HUD to organize R&D on a rational basis, as recommended by the Woods Hole Summer Study, using various incentives to encourage industrial collaboration.

But R&D programs in housing technology continue to encounter difficulties, and Harold Finger, assistant secretary for urban research and technology in HUD, has observed that the construction industry remains unwilling to accept the idea that the necessary research cannot be handled within its present structure.[7] In January 1970 a report by a Department of Commerce panel on housing technology reviewed the obstacles to technological change in the building industry in language almost identical to that of the report on the industry that appeared in the early 1960's.[8] This report recommended that the federal government take the lead in stimulating building

[6] Carroll, *op. cit.* James Carroll, at Ohio State University, is currently undertaking a detailed study of HUD's R&D program.

[7] Harold Finger, "The Goal of Operation Breakthrough," *Journal of Housing,* 26 (December 1969), 587 ff.

[8] U.S. Department of Commerce, *The Housing Industry: A Challenge to the Nation* (Washington, D.C.: GPO, January 1970).

technology and that appropriations of $100 million annually be given HUD to improve building technology. HUD requested $55 million, but in August 1970 the congressional appropriations for the HUD technology effort was only $30 million, low enough to require some cutback in existing activities.[9] And Daniel Greenberg has commented that HUD has yet to develop a significant research effort even at a time when most civilian-oriented departments are increasing their research expenditures.[10]

The Impact of Technology

The potential impact of technology has been a controversial question, in large measure because of the great variety of factors influencing the cost and efficiency of housing production. After World War II the demand for more housing and the increased production capability that had developed during the war stimulated innovation. Prefabrication was, at that time, the technological thrust, but it failed to develop as a significant part of the industry for a number of reasons. The standardization and uniformity necessary for prefabrication coincided with the growth of suburbia and consumer demand for individualized housing. Further, it was found that costs of on-site assembly minimized savings from factory production of parts. Improved methods of construction which would have reduced assembly costs were impeded

[9] *Business Week*, August 8, 1970. For an indication of some of the problems faced by HUD in seeking appropriations, see *New York Times*, February 1, 1970, and June 14, 1970.

[10] *Science and Government Report* 2, February 15, 1971.

by the political activity of those with interests in preserving the existing situation.

Such obstacles continue to be significant, but there are many who consider that today, more than ever, rapid technological change in the industry is necessary, and is perhaps the only way to meet increasing housing needs. They point to population statistics indicating that the baby-boom generation is reaching the age of maximum housing needs, to the deterioration of the slums, and to the decreasing construction-labor pool, which is not replenishing its ranks as it has in past generations. They note that public pressure to respond to housing needs has failed to speed the slow pace of the craft methods that characterize the building industry.[11]

A number of observers argue that the cost reduction from using improved building techniques would not significantly reduce the cost of housing. Continuing expenses of storage and maintenance, land-acquisition problems, and such economic factors as limited market aggregation reduce the impact of technology on housing costs.[12] In addition, an unresolved problem is the seasonal nature of employment in construction, presently compensated by very high hourly wage rates. Significant cost reduction would require a more stable market de-

[11] Joseph Carreiro, *The New Building Block* (Ithaca, N.Y.: Center for Housing and Environmental Studies, Cornell University, 1968), and personal communication, Joseph Carreiro.

[12] Morton J. Schussheim, "Housing in Perspective" *The Public Interest*, 19 (Spring 1970), 18 ff.

mand, or guaranteed minimum commitments to provide stable employment.

On the other hand, the increase in land costs and high population mobility are creating a demand for multi-family units amenable to mass-production methods. This would tend to resolve the market aggregation problems that have long obstructed the application of technology. Those who are optimistic about the possibilities of technological improvement point to the success of the one segment of the housing industry which is technically advanced and industrialized, namely that of mobile homes. In 1965, the retail cost of a mobile home was about $8 per square foot, or less than two-thirds the price of a typical low-price development home. The fact that they are usually financed as motor vehicles rather than with mortgages has also contributed to their popularity. It has been estimated that in 1966, mobile homes provided about 22 per cent of all single-family, nonfarm, privately constructed housing in the United States, and about three-fourths of all new single-family homes that sold for under $12,500.[13]

Advocates of new technology, including Hollomon, look at two dimensions of the housing-production problem: first, the development of industrialized production methods that would approach the problem as an entire system; second, the development of technology in the narrower sense—development of new materials and new ways of using materials. While this narrower dimension

[13] Carreiro, *op. cit.*, p. 28.

of technological development remains important, and there is continuing research on the possibilities of, for example, improved dimensional tolerances and adhesive techniques, the main emphasis is on the organizational aspects of technology.

Technology has its greatest cost-reducing impact in those instances where it can accelerate the building process. . . . If significant cost reduction is to be achieved, greater effort is needed to develop improved techniques for management and decision making.[14]

To date, industrial production methods have had little impact on reducing cost and increasing efficiency, but this is blamed on the "belated degree of organization [which does] not in any way exploit the high quantities of production that the term 'industrialized' suggests when used in relation to other industries."[15] Advocates argue that the relevant technology has not in fact been developed; that production methodology has been too primitive to evaluate cost factors properly. In particular, before evaluation can be made, problems of on-site assembly and distribution have to be worked out.

Crude estimates of the potential benefits of developing industrialized housing may be found by considering the European experience since World War II. The critical

[14] National Academy of Sciences, *Urban Research and Development: Technological Considerations* (Washington, D.C.: GPO, 1969).

[15] Alexander Pike, "Failure of Industrialized Building and Housing Programs," *Architectural Design*, 37(2) (November 1967), 507–508.

dimensions of the building shortage in Europe after the war eliminated many of the obstacles to innovation that have impeded the American building industry. With heavy government subsidy, industrial building systems have been in operation since the war, saving an average 10–15 per cent in cost over conventional building. One survey has indicated that in the United Kingdom new building methods permit an estimated reduction in construction time of 20–35 per cent for projects of between two hundred and five hundred units.

In the Soviet Union, where the extensive use of industrial techniques is not fettered by institutional impediments, there has been continuing experimentation in the technology of production methods. The level of industrialization is suggested by the fact that one Moscow plant alone produces thirty thousand units annually. The number of household dwelling units produced annually in the U.S.S.R. has been twice that produced in the United States, though there has been considerable criticism of quality standards. According to one estimate, however, if the current technology applied in the U.S.S.R. were in wide use in the United States, American industry could produce housing meeting required quality standards for less than half the present cost.[16]

[16] U.S. Congress, Joint Economic Committee, Subcommittee on Urban Affairs, *Industrialized Housing* (Washington D.C.: GPO, 1969), pp. 8–10. For additional information on European housing see *United Nations Industrialization of Building* (E/C.6/70, N.Y. 1967) and International Council of Building, *Innovation in Building* (Amsterdam: Elsevier, 1962).

Technology Transfer

The CITP proposal was concerned with transferring existing technology from the highly sophisticated space and defense industries to civilian industry. Technology transfer has been one of the thrusts of recent experiments in developing housing technology. The most striking experiment in this area, supported by DOD funds, has been at the University of Michigan, where prototype housing modules have been built using a fiberglass filament winding procedure adapted from the fabrication of nose cones of space vehicles.[17] While technically successful the experiment did not develop into a program for passing on the benefits of this technology to the general public.

The final phase of the experiment involved a plan to test the prototype by using the DOD housing-procurement program. The DOD builds about eight to ten thousand housing units per year, and its construction program is not inhibited by housing codes or zoning regulations. It could provide a living laboratory for a controlled experiment on new building specifications and on the usefulness of new technological ideas. Plans were made to develop a large army officers' housing complex, but the Michigan researchers were told by the Department of Defense that there was no money available for the final phase of the experiment, and a proposal was never submitted.

[17] S. Paraskevopoulos, "Research on Potential of Advanced Technology for Housing," Architectural Research Lab, University of Michigan, 1968.

To the present time, DOD housing programs are not systematically used to facilitate large-scale experiments on housing technology. The critical problems of technology transfer—dissemination and application of information—have not been approached on the scale necessary to evaluate the validity of some of the ideas presented in the CITP and other housing-technology proposals.[18]

The flow of knowledge from one sector to another hinges on political receptivity. Prior to World War II, the development of new technology in the defense sector met with a great deal of resistance from Congress and enjoyed minimum public funding. However, the receptivity to new technology shifted with its demonstrated usefulness in wartime. From 1944 to 1947, a new aggressive policy was developed, making available massive public funding for defense R&D channeled primarily through private institutions.[19] In the space sector, the rapidity of technological change lessened the obstructive power of the few long-established vested interests. The space and defense programs have had the benefit of clear objectives, long-range support, and minimal opposition. Their programs have been carried out in a new industry, aerospace, and have involved very little competition with existing interests. Once the policy context was established, research objectives were defined, and the neces-

---

[18] Samuel I. Doctors, *The Role of Federal Agencies in Technology Transfer* (Cambridge, Mass.: M.I.T. Press, 1969).

[19] Clarence H. Danhoff, *Government Contracting and Technological Change* (Washington: Brookings Institution, 1968), Chap. II.

sary technology developed. In this framework, the space and defense industries have demonstrated an ability to resolve complex, multifaceted technological problems with remarkable success.

It is far more difficult to deal with a problem such as housing in the civilian economy. Objectives are vague, opposition is powerful, and support is erratic. "Technology seems to progress most successfully when it fills a vacuum and to encounter the greatest resistance when it tries to penetrate an existing technostructure. It is this factor which makes innovation in the civilian sector most difficult." [20] There are particular problems in an industry such as housing where the technology is based largely on practical experience rather than on research. The situation resembles, in many ways, the process of technology transfer in developing countries, where a network of existing social, political, and economic institutions must be considered. Much depends upon the success with which proponents of an idea can communicate in the political context. The degree to which political receptivity hinges on communication is revealed in the acerbic exchanges between the CITP proponents and the members of the Appropriations Committee.

[20] Personal communication, Harvey Brooks. See also Michael Michaelis, "Obstacles to Innovation," *International Science and Technology*, 35 (November 1964).

V / A Communications Dilemma

The CITP controversy occurred at a time when there was no broad or well-defined policy context in which to propose a government program for developing building technology. In February 1962 the House of Representatives had rejected, by a vote of 264 to 150, a Kennedy-sponsored program which would have created a Cabinet-level Department of Urban Affairs and Housing.[1] No department existed to which the CITP could be attached, as, for example, Operation Breakthrough was later to be tied to HUD.

With no established policy support, a great deal depended on the ability of CITP proponents to communicate persuasively with individual congressmen, especially with those who controlled the budget. Personal style, old suspicions and animosities, and skill in political negotiation—not substantive arguments—were the operative factors, and they limited communication.

Communication on the question of government-

[1] Frederic N. Cleaveland et al., *Congress and Urban Problems* (Washington, D.C.: Brookings Institution, 1969), pp. 173ff.

sponsored civilian research was further inhibited by the general congressional mistrust of the powerful scientific and technical elite whom Kennedy had brought into his administration as advisers. This group of "technocrats" was suggesting new approaches to economic and social problems that involved increased federal activity. Many of their ideas were considered radical at the time and served to aggravate the tenuous nature of congressional-administrative relationships. Congressman Bow, in questioning Hollomon, kept referring to "your scientists," to "those people"; and in examining the CITP Advisory Committee, he noted sarcastically: "You have how many universities? . . . I think you have one [man] from private industry." John Rooney commented on the proposed staffing of the CITP, "mostly all chiefs; very few indians," and continued to refer to "chiefs" throughout the hearings.

Hollomon's style did not allay public mistrust. He exhibited a confidence which limited his adaptability to the political concerns of the Appropriations Committee. Hollomon claimed that he had little political advice; that in the early years of an administration, particularly when a large number of new positions are created, many people new to Washington do not know how to cope with the political scene. This is a time when congressional committees have extraordinary power. Hollomon was one of the new arrivals in Washington. When advice was given him—such as the BOB suggestion to support the program with legislation prior to seeking appropriations—out of inexperience he chose to ignore it. The CITP request was his first confrontation with the Appropriations Committee, and he had not yet developed the art of negotiation.

Underlying the difficulties in communication evident in the CITP case lies a gap between what may be called the logic of technology and that of politics. Each is a highly professional activity based on a distinctive set of assumptions and values, defined boundaries, and characteristic concepts of client responsibility.

The Logic of Technology

Hollomon engaged in politics for a purpose: to sell his program to the Appropriations Committee. His proposal dealt with a substantive issue—the need for technological innovation in lagging industries—and he supported it with technological and economic arguments. But the building industry accused Hollomon of being inadequately informed, and he surely was with respect to the opinions of the industry and the character of Appropriations Committee hearings.

Hollomon arrived at the hearings with strong support from the Kennedy science-policy establishment. As a part of that establishment himself, Hollomon shared its mode of operation, one based on the logic of technology, in which hard facts and a well-articulated purpose have led to the remarkable development of modern science and technology.

A technologist proceeds to solve problems by defining objectives and then making a comprehensive analysis of the most efficient way to reach these objectives. He considers rigorously the available knowedge; but often this knowledge is inadequate for calculating an ideal solution to a problem. He often cannot wait for definitive research to be done. Thus technology depends a great deal on expertise: "There will be a large element of the incalculable, of sheer art, in what he does. . . . Each situation is so complex and has so many unassessable factors, that the only sensible policy . . . is to rely upon skill and experience." [2]

Engineers and scientists often see technology as a solution to a great variety of problems, and try to apply their technological approach to problems outside their professional area. But they often define problems in terms too narrow to do justice to the complexity of real situations, assuming that it is the substantive character of a problem alone which determines the course of action. The technologist does not think it necessary to weigh conflicting interests, but only the relative advantages of various approaches to resolving his problem. Consensus is not sought; the primary responsibility is to a client or, in an area involving scientific research, to professional peers. Thus did Hollomon, confident of the validity of his approach to the problem, present the program to Congress with naïve directness.

Hollomon was slow to acquire the skill of obfuscation, which is an immensely useful one for a government official who is trying to sell a controversial program. . . . He has been variously accused of arrogance and of thinking his

2 J. A. Ziman, *Public Knowledge* (Cambridge: At the University Press, 1968), p. 24.

background has equipped him for developing quick solutions for the complex problems of economic growth . . . [but] it would be closer to the mark to say that at least at first he was not at all inhibited about expressing his thoughts on just why industry and Congress should support the CIT.[3]

Hollomon had little patience with the time perspective of Congress and little inclination for the kinds of political activity required to counter or accommodate the interests of the building industry. His experience in a corporate environment, in which decisions were made in a hierarchical manner, reinforced his tendency to ignore politics and interest groups. But he soon was forced to respond to political realities: that a proposal is rarely judged simply on its own terms; that style of presentation is as much a factor in success as the quality of substance; that often a program is accepted by default— that is, because it involves the least disagreement and the least risk.

Hollomon's initial insensitivity to the concerns of the

[3] *Science*, 140, June 28, 1963. There is a literature dealing with the relationship between scientists and politics. Robert Gilpin notes: "Whereas the politician often seeks to persuade an opponent through appeals to passion, the threat of force, and the use of force, the scientist tends to assume there is one truth to which all reasonable men will accede once its nature has been explained." Robert Gilpin, *American Scientists and Nuclear Weapons Policy* (Princeton: Princeton University Press, 1962), p. 306. See also Joseph Haberer, *Politics and the Community of Science* (New York: Van Nostrand Reinhold, 1969); and Robert Gilpin and Christopher Wright, eds., *Scientists and National Policy Making* (New York: Columbia University Press, 1964).

building industry helped to weaken his own case. Assuming from the beginning that the objections to the CITP could have no legitimate basis, he was unable to anticipate them or respond to them. Once the opposition was public, and clearly of political importance, Hollomon tried to change his approach. Responding to pressure from the industry, he altered his proposal in order to minimize its bearing on proprietary products. But it was strategically too late. When he underplayed product innovation, emphasizing the broader institutional and organizational aspects of technology, he was accused of vagueness and of failing to define the purpose of the program. In trying to see the program on the basis of its intrinsic reasonableness and the legitimacy of its objectives, Hollomon was working, in effect, in terms of a logic hopelessly at odds with that of the congressmen who controlled the purse.

The Logic of Politics

Legislators operate according to "a rough and ready kind of rationality that deals with a tremendous number of variables. . . . It is often best concretized in those overriding compromises that, from the viewpoint of a technocrat or an idealist, seem to be logically absurd." [4] Unlike the technologist, who uses his expertise to define and reach specific technological objectives, the politician seeks to establish a consensus in the context of a large

[4] Bertram M. Gross, "The State of the Nation: Social Systems Accounting," in Raymond Bauer, ed., *Social Indicators* (Cambridge, Mass.: M.I.T. Press, 1966), p. 250.

number of often conflicting pressures. His approach to establishing that consensus depends both on his personal style and on the character of his constituency. Faced with excessive demands, the congressman "indulges in selective perception of what he hears, and . . . [is] prone to express whatever predisposition he has regarding it." [5] Thus the substantive aspect of an issue, of primary concern to the technologist, may be of secondary importance to the legislator.

The logic characteristic of legislators is based on the need to represent public interests. As the fate of the CITP suggests, however, a "rough and ready rationality" may work in the service, not so much of the public interest, as of the political interests of certain highly organized and articulate groups. Political logic dictates that congressmen who are subject to pressure from large and powerful constituent groups respond to such pressure. And it is these groups which are best represented. One consequence of this is considerable institutional inertia, suggesting that the logic of politics may lead to a dangerous myopia. Also, congressmen are constrained to consider among alternative policies "only those relatively few alternatives that represent small or incremental changes from existing policies." [6]

Personal style and rapport may help to influence the

[5] Raymond A. Bauer, Ithiel de Sola Pool, and Lewis Anthony Dexter, *American Business and Public Policy* (New York: Atherton Press, 1963), p. 415.

[6] Charles E. Lindblom, *The Intelligence of Democracy* (New York: Free Press, 1965), p. 144.

logic of politics. For example, Senator Clinton Anderson (Democrat/New Mexico) who, through his membership in the Joint Committee on Atomic Energy, regularly works with scientists, suggests what helps determine congressional support of a technical program. "A politician is someone who has learned that people have interests. . . . He goes around trying to understand what other men want. . . . You just don't define it in easy terms of, is he a politician or isn't he a politician. It's the personal contacts people make."

With respect to those who propose programs, Senator Anderson indicates that personal qualities are as important as the substantive issues. Speaking of a scientist who had come with a request, he says: "I found he had other interests in life besides the scientific interests. He had a family . . . friends . . . and so forth. I decided he was a better sort of person than I thought . . . and anything he asked me for from that time on I tried to do." [7]

Hollomon's personality clearly grated on both John Rooney and Frank Bow. This, in addition to other fortuitous factors, influenced the congressional decision. Participants in the case, even those strongly supportive of the CITP, recall that Hollomon made no secret of his personal attitudes toward the construction industry and toward Congress. Discussion at cocktail parties, well known as a potent element in the political communications network, may well have filtered down to the Appropriations Committee and affected their response.

[7] Clinton B. Anderson, interview, "The Politics of Science," *International Science and Technology*, 28 (April 1964).

Furthermore, the independence of Hollomon's operating style, his failure to consult more than a few people in the industry until after his plans were well established, proved to be a mistake. Hollomon was later to advise others trying to design similar programs not only to sell their ideas to the building industry, but also to include the industry at the planning stage. His own neglect of this strategy—his tendency to work solely in terms of his own logic—contributed to the opposition of the Appropriations Committee.

How does political logic actually work in the Appropriations Committee? A committee is itself a social system with its own norms and patterns of behavior. An analysis of appropriations politics suggests that committees operate on the basis of two norms, clearly understood by all members: first, that the committee objective is to protect the budget; second, that there should be cooperation and consensus on all committee decisions.[8] New members are rapidly socialized to these norms, and it is understood that they are to follow the leadership of the chairman. The position of chairman is a source of considerable power, for tradition generally allows him a great number of decision-making prerogatives. Hollomon believed he had the support of several members of the subcommittee; but none would venture to take issue with Chairman Rooney.

The norms of consensus and unity are reflected in membership stability within the Committee. In 1962,

[8] Richard F. Fenno, *The Power of the Purse* (Boston: Little Brown, 1966), pp. 209 ff.

seven members of the Subcommittee on Deficiencies had served an average of 17.1 years in the House, and the seven members of Rooney's subcommittee had served an average of 10.7 years. Rooney himself has been in Congress since 1944 (see Appendix II).

The inflexible structure of the committee system, reinforcing the logic of politics, clearly operates against innovation and change. In the CITP case, the argument for innovation based on anticipation of future needs was derailed, in part because congressmen tended to respond to building-industry pressure, immediate and articulate.

Hollomon cynically concluded that the only way to get a new technology program through the system is to bypass the normal appropriations route by proposing an agency of such size that, like the Atomic Energy Commission, it creates its own congressional apparatus. To the extent that smaller ventures are successful, their proponents have learned that bridging the communications gap between technology and politics requires considering style and strategy as well as substance. Style, appearances, the manipulation of props, and other factors that are dramaturgical in the world of technologists are a part of the logic of politics. Strategy requires undertaking the long and arduous process of building industrial support, catering to the "pork barrel" syndrome, and generally making accommodations to the pressures, priorities, and predilections of the subcommittee members.

VI / *The Use of Technology*

The CITP proposal called for "a national coordinated research program, interdisciplinary in nature and industry-wide in scope" (see Appendix I). Its recommendations stemmed from a technology-based assumption that an integrated approach is required to resolve social problems.

What is needed in a complex socio-technical matter is a "coherent doctrine"—that is a set of precepts and view points, some from the technological sciences, some from social sciences, some not from science but rather drawn from common sense and experience, that constitutes a rational, integrated approach to the problem.[1]

It was just this "coherent doctrine" that building-industry spokesmen found unpalatable. For, as indicated in Table 8, their views on the state of the industry, technology, and the role of the federal government were

[1] Alvin M. Weinberg, "Social Problems and National Socio-technical Institutes" in National Academy of Sciences, *Applied. Science and Technological Progress* (Washington, D.C.: GPO, 1967, p. 427).

based on a totally different set of assumptions. It remains to analyze the factors that prompted the building industry's opposition to the CITP and made possible the industry's domination of the political process.

Table 8. The CITP controversy

Issues	Arguments	
	CITP supporters	*CITP opponents*
State of the building industry	Lagging and technologically obsolete	Productive and economically sound
Innovation	Impossible within a traditional industry, such as construction, except by "invasion" from other industries	Occurs within industry as dictated by the marketplace
The transfer of technology from space and defense to the civilian sector	A necessary component of economic development	Threatening to existing economic balance between private and public sectors
Housing needs	Impossible to meet without radical change in technology	Within current technological capability of industry
Public funding of construction industry research	Necessary to reduce building costs and to meet public needs	Threatening to free enterprise
Current federal funding activities	Out of balance, insufficient funding of civilian technology	Overextended in all sectors

First of all, a stable and well-established system may be particularly resistant to social change.

The various forms of corporate resistance to change which reflect themselves as obstacles to technological innovation are processes of conservatism essential to the survival of any social and biological organism. . . . It is the crisis of modern industrial corporations that they are also required to undertake technical change destructive of their stable states in order to survive. It is this paradox which . . . accounts for their ambivalence to innovation.[2]

The character of technology in the building industry, emphasizing craft methods rather than science-based techniques, operates against innovation. Industrialized building techniques are not only commercially disruptive; they also threaten the traditional assumption that building methods are developed through a long history of empirical experience.

As important an obstacle to change is the fact that inefficiency and costly design are rewarding to the many diverse segments of the industry. There is little incentive for technological competence which might lead to cost reduction; indeed, there is a certain stake in maintaining inefficiencies, particularly in view of the industry's highly competitive character. The introduction of new technology would upset the existing competitive balance. In this light, government support of a building-research

[2] Donald A. Schon, *Technology and Change* (New York: Delta, 1967), p. 73.

program was looked upon as an *intervention* rather than as a *subsidy*. Hollomon underestimated the importance of competition in the industry and consequently the intensity of the response.

The CITP met further opposition because of its implications for the highly sensitive issue of resource allocation. Technological innovation in the private economy tends to develop in response to market demands, on the assumption that this will lead to an appropriate allocation of resources. But market mechanisms have failed to generate innovation where it is necessary to meet expanding housing needs. This raises a vexing question. On the one hand, housing is a private good, since it is consumed by individuals. On the other, the high cost of housing, in part attributable to the inefficiency and technological conservatism of the building industry, has placed adequate shelter out of reach of many people. Since social values place a high priority on adequate shelter, housing becomes essentially a public good; a public response is required when individual needs are not met by the private market.[3] As one economist has

[3] Harvey Brooks has called my attention to this issue. A brief note on the distinction between the "public" and the "private" good is useful. Many economists define the public good in terms of collective consumption: a good is public "if X's consumption of it leads to no subtraction from what is left over for consumption by Y and Z." See Francis M. Bator, *The Question of Government Spending: Public Needs and Private Wants* (New York: Harper, 1960). A broader definition attempts to include situations where the market has failed to produce desired goods by defining a public good as one in which there is "(1) an appreciable difference in either quantity or quality between

noted, "In the absence of public policy, there is nothing automatic about the system of incentives and institutions allocating R&D resources which generates an optimal allocation." [4] Those who would clearly gain from innovation in building, low-income consumers, are poorly organized to express their needs; and there are few mechanisms through which affected interests can be brought into decisions concerning technological application.

When a new and less costly building technique would disrupt the construction industry, one can rely on the opposition of those building interests that would be disadvantaged, but not on organized advocacy by residents of the ghetto who might benefit from cheaper housing. In these and similar situations, a thorough consideration of the relative merits of alternative technologies is rendered difficult if not impossible by the presence of powerful spokesmen for the old

------

[a collective good] and the alternatives the private market would produce and (2) a viable demand for the difference." This broader definition would allow for the ambiguous distinction between "public" and "private" with respect to housing. See Peter O. Steiner, "The Public Sector and the Public Interest," U.S. Congress, Joint Economic Committee, *The Analysis and Evaluation of Public Expenditures: The PPB System* (Washington, D.C.: GPO, 1969). This article contains a review of various distinctions between public and private. See also Edmund S. Phelps, ed., *Private Wants and Public Needs,* (New York: Norton, 1962).

[4] Richard R. Nelson, "Technological Advance, Economic Growth and Public Policy," Walter Heller, *Perspectives on Economic Growth* (New York: Random House, 1968), pp. 187–208.

technologies, and the absence of effective spokesmen for the new.[5]

Finally, opposition to the CITP developed from a general concern with government spending which was increasing in all sectors. For example, a *Fortune* editorial of 1963 said:

Nothing in the record suggests that government organizes research more efficiently than industry can do it. . . . The way to right a listing vessel is not always to add more cargo to the upside. Sometimes the job can be done by jetissoning some junk from the downside. We recommend that Commerce forget about the CIT Program while NASA and Defense get going on cuts. Thus balance can be improved while saving money instead of by blowing more of it.[6]

The success of the opposition to the CITP reflects the dominance of interest groups in the political process. We have seen several ways in which these groups used their political power to resist change. Despite the fragmented character of the construction industry, a relatively small number of people formed an "invisible college" controlling the various organizations which are part of the industrial network. In addition to the political power inherent in this network, the industry was able to base its position on clearly defined economic interests that were meaningful to congressmen. Overburdened legislators tend to favor safe and noncontroversial decisions

[5] National Academy of Sciences, *Technology: Processes of Assessment and Choice*, Committee on Science and Astronautics, U.S. House of Representatives, July 1969, p. 40.

[6] Editorial, *Fortune Magazine*, May 1963, p. 104.

involving minimal risk. The concerns of the industry were therefore more cogent in the political framework than the ambitious, yet uncertain objectives of the CITP. Hollomon's personal style in presenting these objectives reinforced congressional attitudes, and was a decisive factor in the success of industrial interests.

The position of the building industry with respect to federal funding of research developed out of historical relationships between industry and government in the United States.

We have lived for generations in a climate of prevailing mutual distrust between industry and government. This distrust has its roots in our revolutionary origins and has grown in a climate of increased federal responsibility and regulatory control which began in the time of the New Deal.[7]

Arguments used against the CITP proposal for encouraging government-industry collaboration were similar to those raised against public education in the 1880's and against welfare in the 1960's.

Since the CITP case, the relationship between government and the private sector has changed considerably in response to a number of obvious and compelling crises. Many of the ideas concerning government activity that at the time were considered radical are now accepted; and in fact, many of the specific proposals of the CITP were implemented several years later within the Department of Commerce. The Institute of Applied Technol-

____
[7] Schon, *op. cit.*, p. 187.

ogy (IAT) was created during a reorganization of the National Bureau of Standards in 1964, and John Eberhard, who had been an adviser to Hollomon during the CITP controversy, was responsible for its construction program. Aware of the political problems, he sought support of the building industry prior to implementing any activities.

In 1965, the State Technical Services Act laid the basis of an extension program creating a network of information centers in universities to serve the technical needs of local firms. This program implemented parts of the CITP and opposition was avoided through the maintenance of close ties with industry. The program was terminated in 1969, however, when Mr. Rooney succeeded in severing its appropriations.

HUD building-research programs have incorporated incentives for industrial participation. But realizing the difficulties of penetrating the existing structure of the building industry, HUD has tended to bypass it in favor of large manufacturing firms: "The whole damn building group sees Breakthrough as a plot by big industry to take over business at government expense." [8] Despite such criticism, HUD's efforts to develop a coordinated program have also evoked some positive action from private industry, if only in response to the threat of increased government activity. Segments of the industry, manufacturers of building products in particular, have been prodded to rethink questions of production efficiency and, in some cases, to support the technological effort of

[8] *Newsweek*, June 22, 1970, p. 74.

HUD "even though it could seriously affect our business way of life. . . . [For] government which represents the public will move in when private business leaves a big enough vacuum long enough." [9]

Despite increased if reluctant acceptance of public programs, federal involvement in civilian technology remains largely responsive to immediate crises such as war and riots, or in some cases to visible economic decline in a particular area. Then problem-solving is approached by declaring "war"—on poverty, against hunger, to save the environment—rather than by instituting procedures through which domestic needs can be routinely perceived and coherently resolved. Undramatic, systematic research and development designed to *avoid* crises, tends to be neglected. The process by which political decisions were made concerning the CITP illustrates how the fate of such programs hangs on fortuitous forces: the crisis of the moment, the personal style of a program's protagonist, or congressional responsiveness to pressures from groups concerned with their own perpetuation. In the absence of more representative procedures, decisions as to R&D priorities in civilian technology will continue to be made on a crisis basis, limiting the extent to which science and technology can be relevant to the resolution of complex domestic problems.

[9] Douglas Grymes, president, Koppers Co., Inc., "Building from Bedlam to Truck Bed," Address at Annual Meeting of the Producers' Council, September 16, 1970.

Appendix I / CITP Proposal on the Technology of Building[1]

Building is the largest industry in the United States, involving $80 billion yearly and accounting for one-sixth of the gross national product.

As a vital organ in the nation's economic body, its well-being directly affects the economic health of the country. Overall growth is not possible unless the building industry keeps pace.

Looking forward, economic predictions call for a total output of structures before the end of this century at least equal to our total current inventory, exclusive of replacements and major innovations.

Like textiles, building too has been recognized by the National Academy of Sciences and the Panel on civilian Technology as an industry needing Federal support of research to define its problems and devise solutions.

The building industry is highly fragmented and local in character. In its housing component, which dollarwise accounts for a third of the industry, no single builder ac-

[1] Subcommittee on Deficiencies, 87th Congress, *op. cit.*, pp. 48–49.

counts for more than 5,000 units and most builders erect fewer than 20 houses a year.

No single group is responsible for building science and technology, nor is there an interdisciplinary, industrywide, scientific tradition, scientific literature, or professional corps. The building research now going on in the United States (and it is considerable) is being done by groups with special interests to serve—the Government to support the specific projects or problems of its agencies; industry to further product development and application; the research performed by academic and nonprofit professional organizations is limited by available funds and personnel, and is channeled mostly into programs sponsored by industry and Government on an ad hoc basis.

The industry's problems are becoming more acute. Technology affecting it is increasing in both quantity and degree of sophistication, and the gap between technological potential and actual building practice is widening. The broadening of our markets from national and regional to world wide brings with it both sharper competitive challenge and greater opportunity, particularly with respect to the European Common Market.

A nationally coordinated research program, interdisciplinary in nature and industrywide in scope is needed.

The following is proposed:

(a) *Encourage and support building science and technology centers in colleges and universities.*—These centers are to be interdisciplinary not only within the physical sciences but in the arts as well, including esthetic, social, and economic fields.

Government support would take the form of research and contracts to selected institutions that have latent capabilities in building science and technology. This will develop a nucleus of trained professionals who can transfer their know-how to others and who can be of immediate assistance to members of the construction industry in nearby areas.

(b) *Building research and development contracts.*—The research and development would be directed toward (1) developing and establishing criteria for the evaluation of new materials, new building components, and new concepts of building technology so that innovations may be effectively and quickly applied; (2) further development and refinement of the modular concept so as to facilitate interchange between the metric and English systems (important to an expanded international trade) and to exploit the potentialities of interchangeability of building components and parts in the domestic market; (3) collecting data not feasibly collected by private industry but important enough for Government to do so—viz., soil analyses and profiles to provide benchmarks to guide construction and land development; and (4) studying the probable course of future technological progress and its impact. The research will not duplicate, but will supplement, the work of other agencies on related subjects, such as air pollution, water supply, sewage systems.

As a part of an industry-university technical service, the building science and technology centers will serve as convenient sources of information and guidance for builders, planners and material suppliers.

In addition, the research will indicate what is technologically possible, economically feasible, and esthetically acceptable in the building industry. The approach will be a systems one with the structure considered as a whole rather than by segment. Moreover, the study will be unfettered by existing practices, codes, and regulations; it will seek to determine the ideal shelter for man's needs, whether that be a home, a factory, a public building, or any other structure. It will assess the capability of present technology to provide that ideal shelter, and indicate what technical developments in the future are needed and possible to achieve the goal.

The research and development in these areas will be carried out on contract by Government agencies (such as the National Bureau of Standards, Bureau of the Census), non-profit research groups, and other research institutions.

(c) *Improve the dissemination of information on building science and technology.*—Improvement of communication on two levels—the professional and the layman—is an essential ingredient in the program.

The development of a technical literature with a scientific tradition, such as professional journals, will be encouraged to meet the needs of building scientists, architects, and engineers. This will provide the important interchange of information among colleagues working in the building field.

The fragmented and local character of the industry means that individual firms do not have the trained staff to search, interpret, and apply the technical literature effectively. Therefore, also proposed are dissemination of technological information in such a form that the businessman can make quick and effective use of it and utilization and expansion of the industry-university technical service.

Appendix II / *Appropriations Subcommittee Membership, 1962*[1]

Subcommittee on Deficiences of the Committee on Appropriations, House of Representatives, 87th Congress:

Name	Party/state	Entered Congress
Albert Thomas, Chairman	Democrat/Texas	1/3/37
Michael J. Kirwan	Democrat/Ohio	1/3/37
Ben F. Jensen	Republican/Iowa	1/3/39
John J. Rooney	Democrat/New York	6/6/44
Frank T. Bow	Republican/Ohio	1/3/51
Edward P. Boland	Democrat/Massachusetts	1/3/53
Charles Raper Jonas	Republican/North Carolina	1/3/53

Subcommittee on Appropriations for the Departments of State, Justice and Commerce, House of Representatives, 88th Congress:

[1] *Congressional Directory* (Washington, D.C.: GPO)

Name	*Party/state*	*Entered Congress*
John J. Rooney, Chairman	Democrat/New York	6/6/44
Robert L. F. Sikes	Democrat/Florida	11/5/40
Frank T. Bow	Republican/Ohio	1/3/51
Glenard P. Lipscomb	Republican/California	11/10/53
Elford A. Cederberg	Republican/Michigan	1/3/53
John M. Slack	Democrat/West Virginia	1/3/59
Neal Smith	Democrat/Iowa	1/3/59

Appendix III / Members of the Building Industry Advisory Board to the CIT Program

Appointed by the National Academy of Sciences[1]

Chairman

John A. Robertson, director of technical services, Washington, United States Gypsum Co., 1011 Arlington Boulevard, Arlington, Va.

Members

Alan E. Brockbank, Alan E. Brockbank Organizations, Post Office Box 1499, Salt Lake City, Utah.

James W. Cawdrey, Cawdrey & Vemo, Inc., 3601 Fremont Avenue, Seattle, Wash.

Stuart Davis, chairman, First Savings & Loan Association of Oakland, 1700 Broadway, Oakland, Calif.

[1] Subcommittee on Departments of State, Justice and Commerce of the Committee on Appropriations, U.S. Senate, 88th Congress, *Hearings* (Washington, D.C.: GPO, 1964) Part 2, p. 2389. There was a separate advisory board for the Textile Program.

Albert G. H. Dietz, professor of building construction, Department of Civil & Sanitary Engineering, Massachusetts Institute of Technology, Cambridge, Mass.

Douglas Greenwald, chief economist, McGraw-Hill Book Co., 330 West 42d Street, New York, N.Y.

C. J. Haggerty, president, Building & Construction Trades Department, AFL-CIO, 815 16th Street, Washington, D.C.

Joseph Newman, general manager, Tishman Research Corp., 666 Fifth Avenue, New York, N.Y.

Alwin B. Newton, vice president and director of research, York Corp., York, Pa.

Gerald F. Prange, vice president for technical services, National Lumber Manufacturers Association, 1619 Massachusetts Avenue, Washington, D.C.

Raymond C. Reese, Raymond C. Reese Associates, Box 556, Toledo, Ohio.

Herbert H. Swinburne, Nolen, Swinburne & Associates, 1601 Locust Street, Philadelphia, Pa. (AIA Research Committee chairman).

Robert B. Taylor, director, Structural Clay Products Research Foundation, Geneva, Ill.

Thomas E. Werkema, program manager, construction materials, Plastics Department, Dow Chemical Co., Midland, Mich.

Appendix IV / *Building Research Advisory Board, 1962*[1]

Frederick M. Babcock, appraiser, Frederick M. Babcock & Co., Washington, D.C.

Max Barth, Chief, Technical Division, Directorate of Construction, Office of the Assistant Secretary of Defense, Department of Defense, Washington, D.C.

A. Allan Bates, University Valley campus, New York University, Sterling Forest, Tuxedo, N.Y., and National Bureau of Standards, Department of Commerce.

Welton D. Becket, president, Welton Becket & Associates, Los Angeles, Calif.

Glenn H. Beyer, director, Housing Research Center, Cornell University, Ithaca, N.Y.

Alan E. Brockbank, Alan E. Brockbank Organization, Salt Lake City, Utah.

[1] Subcommittee on Departments of State, Justice and Commerce of the Committee on Appropriations, U.S. Senate, 88th Congress, *Hearings* (Washington, D.C.: GPO, 1964) Part 2, pp. 2389–91.

Walter E. Campbell, FAIA, Campbell & Aldrich, Boston, Mass.

Albert G. H. Dietz, professor of building construction, Department of Civil & Sanitary Engineering, Massachusetts Institute of Technology, Cambridge, Mass.

William Gillett, William Gillett Associates, Detroit, Mich.

Peter B. Gordon, vice president, Wolff & Munier, Inc., New York, N.Y.

Ira H. Hardin, president, Ira H. Hardin Co., Atlanta, Ga.

Raymond H. Harrell, executive vice president and director of research, Lumber Dealers Research Council, Washington, D.C.

Malcolm C. Hope, assistant chief, Division of Environmental Engineering and Food Protection, U.S. Public Health Service, Department of Health, Education and Welfare, Washington, D.C.

Alfred L. Jaros, Jr., partner, Jaros, Baum & Bolles, New York, N.Y.

James T. Lendrum, head, Department of Architecture, University of Florida, Gainesville, Fla.

Robert W. Long, partner and president, Long Construction Co., Kansas City, Mo.

Robinson Newcomb, consulting economist, Washington, D.C.

John S. Parkinson, director of general research, Research Center, Johns-Manville Products Corp., Manville, N.J.

Douglas E. Parson, chief, Building Research Division, National Bureau of Standards, Department of Commerce, Washington, D.C.

John A. Robertson, director of product development, United States Gypsum Co., Des Plaines, Ill.

J. D. Rollins, president, American Bridge Division, United States Steel Corp., Pittsburgh, Pa.

Philip C. Rutledge, Moran, Proctor, Mueser & Rutledge, New York, N.Y.

Richard H. Tatlow III, president, Abbot, Merkt & Co., New York, N.Y.

Robert B. Taylor, director, Structural Clay Products Research Foundation, Geneva, Ill.

Max Wehrly, director, Urban Land Institute, Washington, D.C.

Ernest Weissman, assistant director, Bureau of Social Affairs, United Nations, New York, N.Y.

Thomas E. Werkema, industrial research analyst, executive research staff, Dow Chemical Co., Midland, Mich.

Willard Worth, director of research, National Homes Corp. Lafayette, Ind.

Harry B. Zachrison, Sr., supervisory general engineer, Office of the Chief of Engineers, Department of the Army, Washington, D.C.

A Note on the Program on Science, Technology, and Society

The Cornell University Program on Science, Technology, and Society is an interdisciplinary program for teaching, research, and increased public understanding. It evolved from a concern with how scientific discovery and technological innovation are changing economic and political institutions and are altering the values that influence social behavior. The program is funded by the National Science Foundation, the Sloan Foundation, the Henry Luce Foundation, and Cornell University.

This book is the second in a series developed within the program to provide information on scientific and technological advances and on the ways in which important decisions about them are made. Each study deals with a specific case selected to reveal the complexity of situations in which the problems and challenges of technology are an issue, and each study treats in detail the broader implications of the individual case.

A number of common themes will be emphasized throughout the series: the use of science and technology to meet public needs, incentives and constraints on the direction of scientific and technological development, and the control of unintended and undesirable consequences of science and technology. We shall consider, in relation to each of these themes, the social and political behavior of various groups: scientists and technologists in the political-governmental system acting in situations which carry them beyond their technical expertise; legislators and policy makers, forced to make decisions often on the basis of inconclusive evidence; and the public, concerned with the implications of technology, whose interest and activities are likely to bear increasingly on public policy.

FRANKLIN A. LONG, Director
RAYMOND BOWERS, Deputy Director

Abbreviations

AIA—American Institute of Architects
ASCE—American Society of Civil Engineers
BOB—Bureau of the Budget
BRAB—Building Research Advisory Board
BRI—Building Research Institute
CEA—Council of Economic Advisors
CITP—Civilian Industrial Technology Program
DOD—Department of Defense
HHFA—Housing and Home Finance Agency
HUD—Department of Housing and Urban Development
IAT—Institute of Applied Technology of the Department
   of Commerce
IBA—Investing Builders Association
NAS–NRC—National Academy of Sciences, National
   Research Council
NBS—National Bureau of Standards of the Department of
   Commerce
R&D—Research and Development

Index